ALL I AM

ALL I AM

A True Story
of Life's Successes,
Failures, Giving
Back and Salvation

ROBERT M. DUGAN

ISBN: 979-8-89316-398-8 - Paperback
ISBN: 979-8-89316-399-5 - Hardcover
ISBN: 979-8-89316-397-1 - eBook

CONTENTS

FOREWARD

This is a book I never wanted to write.

If not for the unexpected death of Susan, my life's love and soulmate, this book would not have seen the light of day.

Many people have asked me to consider writing about the life I have lived because of the twists and turns and the people who have helped me along the way. I had little interest in talking about myself, no matter how intriguing my life has been. Losing Susan changed that when another world appeared around me. I prayed to Jesus for direction and eventually he responded - rather forcefully. He instructed me to write the book about my life, then add a second account of everything that I would observe and encounter after Susan's death.

As a scientist, I am always digging into and trusting data and graphs. Throughout my life, I have always had a heart filled with empathy for others. The science-based world I thought I knew changed after May 26, 2023, the day I lost Susan. The events and visions that followed Susan's death were beyond hard data, chance or coincidence.

Writing this book will be a reminder to me, and maybe a few readers, how strange life can be, sometimes even unfair. However, as I have had to look back at seventy years of life, I can see there was a plan. Not my own mind you, but that of a much higher power.

My thoughts, intellect, and understanding of the world at my age at that time shaped each chapter that I wrote. Later chapters, when I am smarter and more mature, reflect on some of these life encounters and explain how they affected my life. I call these life lessons.

I write this book to help those undergoing challenges in their careers and lives, hoping to help everyone understand the importance of personal and spiritual relationships, both professionally and socially. My hope is that by the end of this journey with you, I will help those on the fence with their relationship with God and Jesus, that they will come to believe Jesus is real and lives within each one of us and will always be there to help. Is there a living Heaven? I believe there is, and proof will come later in the book.

This book is a dedication to Susan and Jesus Christ. I hope I make them both proud. If I help only one person to believe in what comes during this life and the next, I will be successful! However, I believe Jesus prefers I reach into the hearts of millions!

PART ONE

CHAPTER 1

IN THE BEGINNING

This story of life is one of challenge, failure, success, love, death, Heaven and blessings.

The first blessing arrived on February 1, 1953, in Troy, New York. It was a cold winter day with temperatures dropping below twenty degrees in the afternoon, with winds howling up to forty miles an hour. Of course, being in the hospital, I was sheltered from the weather and had no idea what winter was all about. What I also did not know is that I was waiting for some loving parents to claim this puny kid as I was put up for adoption! I am forever grateful that abortion was not an option in those days, otherwise I may have been murdered before I ever got started on this journey. It is a blessing that babies don't know the workings of life's entanglements.

Blessing number two was having been adopted by two wonderful, smart, and successful individuals. My new dad was Walter J. Dugan, a chemical engineer working for General Electric in Waterford, New York. My new mom, Grace Kennedy Dugan, worked as an executive secretary at Bear Manning in Troy. I would be the second of three adopted children by the Dugans. Later in life, my dad told me that the reason for their choice to adopt a family was because during the war in the Pacific, he was on a ship and witnessed an atomic bomb test and believed the radiation he was subject to could cause deformed or abnormal babies. Little did they know they adopted an unusual child in the process!

I was an early walker and before the end of my second year on this planet, mom and dad noticed I was falling too many times. At first, they thought it was because I was on my feet too soon for someone my age. The truth of my disability, my first curse encountered in my life, was that I had contracted polio, manifested in my left leg. The Salk vaccine had been released in 1953, but I had not gotten the jab yet. As I got older, I was not as fast as the other kids, but I was well-coordinated. For so many years, I blamed God for cursing me at such a young age and continued cursing him over the years whenever I failed anything in life. I would always apologize to God for these curses directed towards Him, but for many years, I kept blaming Him for everything bad and thanking Him for everything good.

Looking back at the polio curse later in life, I believe it was the third blessing perfectly disguised. It only took me forty-three years to understand His master plan.

When I was five or six, my parents sent me to day camp, apparently to get me out of the house. Camp Ca-Da-Ka was a small Jewish camp in the Grafton mountains, about an hour from our house. We learned to ride horses, play kickball and fish in the small lake surrounded by trees. I loved that place. My mother would make me sardine sandwiches for lunch because I loved sardines. The sandwiches were good, but after sitting on the hot bus all day, after the mayonnaise and fish oils soaked into the bread, they really became tasty and smelly! My mom was told to stop making sardine sandwiches for me because the other children were getting ill smelling the fish on the ride home. Well, that was the end of my favorite packed lunch. My dad could not believe I didn't get sick eating that old, smelly fish.

My dad always wanted me to be an engineer, like himself. When I was eight or nine, he purchased an erector set for me. My job was to build a bridge. I remember working hard to make a great bridge without any plans. When I finished, I proudly showed my dad what I had created. He did not like it at all and told me to try again. For the first time in my life, I lost my temper and destroyed my wonderful creation. That was to be an ongoing theme; my quick, destructive temper.

Foot Note: Poliomyelitis is a virus that attacks nerve cells, causing paralysis. Many people died from this awful disease and many, like me, suffered various degrees of paralysis. This disease most frequently affects children under the age of five. My survival with relatively minimal permanent effects was yet another blessing.

Me in 1958 at 5 years old

Sue at 5 years old

CHAPTER 2

THE FIRST
FOURTEEN YEARS

My life as a child was not anything out of the ordinary. Or so I thought at the time. I rode my bicycle everywhere with my pain in the butt dog Rascal following me. I especially enjoyed going to the Poestenkill creek to fish. The moving clear water and the fast-paced minnows held my attention. I enjoyed seeing how these fish always positioned themselves behind rocks in slack water. Then, without notice, darting out to catch a small morsel of food. I never caught many fish there but got whacked by dad when I returned because I was playing by the dangerous water against his commands. Those whacks were worth the many trips I made to my river sanctuary. Fishing remained a major draw in my entire life, as did being on the water.

My friends Frankie and Billy loved playing cowboys and Indians. Our bikes were our horses. Our imaginations directed our playtime. One day, and not one I am proud of, we decided Billy had broken the law and his sentence was death by hanging. Thank God a nice lady was watching us enforce the sentence, because she stopped us from stringing up Billy on a branch with a rope around his neck. The branch was too small to hold his weight, but we almost hung him! I will never forget that day and the intervention by a neighbor. Blessings often come when we need them most, but least expect them.

Frankie and I also loved exploring, always with Rascal close behind. On the nearby road to the Country Club of Troy, there was a large cave about one hundred yards from the road. Frankie and I would go into the dark cave looking for the monster that we knew lived deep inside. Rascal would never go in with us but would bark whenever we entered the monster's home. We figured if the dog barked, the creature that made this dark place his home would surely be there. We never found him and our parents never knew what dangerous places their kids frequently visited.

Baseball became an addiction as well. I loved playing the game and was quite good as my quick hands and strong arm allowed me to pitch, play third base and shortstop. In the days of my youth, my lack of speed did not matter because kids in little league baseball were slow and clumsy by nature. I loved the Yankees because my uncle, Jeff Davis, was a radio announcer for the team. My life of baseball would undergo a dramatic change when my dad got transferred to Plastics (GE) in Pittsfield, Massachusetts. On a side note, my dad's expertise was in taking under-performing sectors of General Electric and resurrecting them. While in Pittsfield, dad managed a group of engineers, including Jack Welch. As a child, I knew Jack, and after my dad was transferred back to GE Silicones in Waterford, New York, Jack bought our house in Pittsfield.

My mother was a tough but insightful lady. She knew that baseball would be a dead end for me and introduced me to many new activities. I began snow skiing, playing the piano, enrolled at the Berkshire Music Conservatory, and playing golf. I expanded my love of fishing, including teaching myself fly-fishing and bass fishing. Being older and more responsible, I never got whacked for going to the lake or river.

The Berkshire Music Conservatory was the place to learn how to read and play classical music. I was too young to appreciate the classics and after two years, and a new teacher with purple hair, I skipped class one night. That should have been worse than getting whacked for fishing! My mom seemed to understand my real musical needs and introduced me to John Galetti, who taught me jazz and rock and roll. Now I was a happy musician playing fun music. I will admit that learning to read music helped that transition. With his teaching, I was now playing the Beatles, Elton John, and the Beach Boys at will. Music is yet another blessing in my life.

I did not mind the cold and took to skiing quickly. I loved the way skis worked and their interaction on the New England ice. I raced and skied the expert trails, falling in love with the mountains.

After breaking my leg at Magic Mountain in Vermont, my racing days were over. Polio affected me in my left leg so appropriately, I broke my left leg. A girl I liked motivated me. Her name was Alynn, and she became a ski instructor at the Bousquet Ski area in Pittsfield. I convinced the ski school director, Court McDermott, to hire me. He was demanding and made every instructor take his lessons on form and precision because he wanted each of his instructors to be the best skiers on the mountain. I benefitted from all those free lessons. I could have taught advanced classes but taught beginners and enjoyed teaching and seeing them advance.

That is when I first experienced my love of teaching! By the time I left Pittsfield, I had become a member of the PSIA, the Professional Ski Instructors of America, at age 14.

Of all the sports I had to play as a child, golf was the real deal. I played all summer with my friends Randy and Scott at Pittsfield Country Club, sometimes playing fifty-four holes a day. By the age of thirteen, I was regularly shooting under eighty. I was even allowed to play in the men's club championship. One year, I played with Robert Jones, the great Bobby Jones's nephew. I never won the club championship, but the experience was encouraging. In retrospect, Pittsfield became the birthplace for everything I do today. Thanks mom, you were the best!

Sports and music weren't the only hobbies in which I took part. I was a choirboy and a horrible altar boy. I could never remember where on the altar I was supposed to stand. After I had broken my leg while in the full leg cast for a second time, Father Dion came to my hospital to help me spiritually through the pain and anger I was feeling for being so stupid. That was the moment I came to see Jesus as a friend, not just as a God.

Everyone has a favorite teacher from school. My ninth-grade biology teacher, Mr. Barber, was the best. He taught biology. He helped me love learning this subject and my grade showed it. I realized I was not stupid but needed a subject I enjoyed to capture my attention. This understanding of my mind would help in future years.

At fifteen, my dad's transfer back to Waterford was about to bring more changes to my life. I was never a talented student but enjoyed, and understood, geometry and physics. Go figure. The change of schools from public to private provided a significant steppingstone to my future.

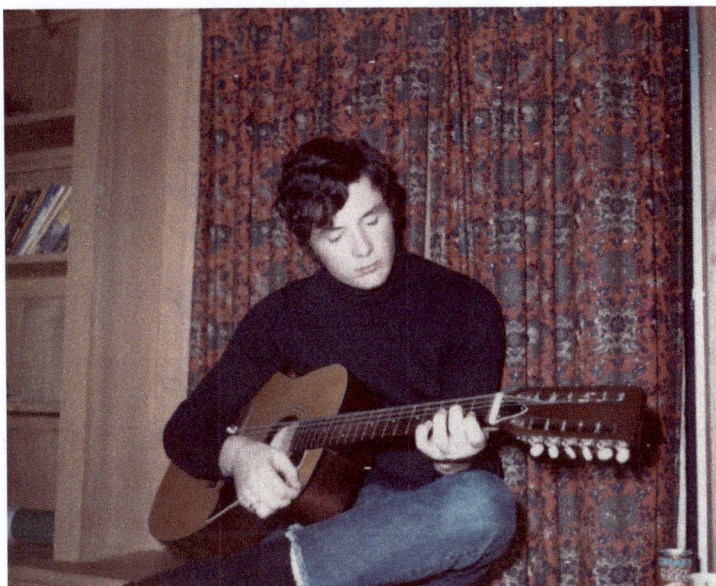

Me with guitar in 1968

CHAPTER 3

THE TRANSITION

General Electric transferred my dad back to Waterford, for a second time, to resurrect the Silicones Division. I was halfway through my sophomore year at Pittsfield High School, where I was a C student, and needed to choose a new school in Troy, New York.

The choice was easy because LaSalle Institute, a Christian Brothers Military academy, was the school my dad and several uncles attended. My dad was the cadet colonel, the top dog. I made the choice, and no, they didn't send me there because I was a bad boy, although I wasn't the most well-behaved. In fact, on my first day in school, Brother Patrick, nicknamed "Doomer", nailed me for cracking up in class. A face slap I never wanted to endure again. However, the rest of my class respected me after that incident.

LaSalle was exactly the environment I needed. I studied harder and frequently made gold or silver honors. I played on the golf team and won the Catholic League Championship in 1970. Most of our matches were match play, a format I came to love and appreciate. I made many friends during this time, many of whom I played against competitively. Mr. Maxwell was our coach and, believe it or not, we drove him crazy. For two and one-half seasons, we seldom lost a team match. Man, I enjoyed winning - and got used to it. The only obstacle was my temper. This weakness was an issue I would have to address later in life.

My nature directed me to form teams that made me happy socially and made use of my athletic skills. So, of course, I had to start a ski team. There were some great skiers at the school, and all they needed was some professional coaching. Here I am! We competed in many high school events and had a lot of fun. We even skied in the world high school championships at Whiteface Mountain in upstate New York. That was a blast, but we were over-matched. It really didn't matter because we discovered beer on that trip. I loved high-level competition and the camaraderie that comes only with competition.

My Aunt Ruth and Uncle Jim Maloy wanted to introduce me to their close friend's daughter, Barbara. A date was arranged, so I had to decide what we would do. Having never been on an official date, I was creative. I found a rock concert scheduled to take place at the Palace Theater in downtown Albany. I did not know who the Who was, but I got tickets. We watched Roger Daltry windmilling his mike, Pete Townshend jumping up and down, Keith Moon killing his drums and John Entwistle hardly moving. Their performance of Tommy rocked my musical world. The Who would become my favorite group, seeing them at least ten times in concert. Live music, in all forms, became my entertainment of choice.

A few years before I started writing this book, my wife and I attended the funeral of a close friend of my folks. I ran into Barbara at the wake, where we briefly conversed. I reminded her that our first and only date was that Who concert. She did not remember going with me. I walked away from her being grateful that I had a fantastic, life-changing date with myself.

Besides skiing and golf and while my leg was still strong, I played tag football, volleyball and intramural basketball. I fell in love with sports and competition. However, the strict nature of the educational-driven Brothers helped me enjoy studying and reading as well. My grades excelled. Without their help and the change from public to private school, I would never have attended Holy Cross College in Worcester, Massachusetts.

I would be remiss if I did not tell you my parents were happy that their son may have a future after all.

Each summer, I worked in the men's clothing department at Montgomery Wards. Strange department for a guy with no taste in clothing, style, or colors. I did like selling terrible ties to unsuspecting men looking for something to match their suits. Oh yea, remember suits?

These summers also gave me the time to compete in the Eastern New York Golf Association weekly golf events open to all ages and flighted by handicaps. Because I carried a two-handicap throughout high school, I always played in the championship division against some very talented players. Many of these talented players became long-time friends. Even some old guys in their thirties!

It was also beneficial for my golf game that my dad joined Albany Country Club when we moved back to New York. A very difficult golf course with two fantastic golf professionals, Bob Mix and Bill Conway, with whom I would remain friends to this day. We would get together at every PGA show just to talk. The way these and other friendships made me feel became the one benefit I treasure the most.

Looking beyond high school graduation with a lot of prayers and thoughts, I applied to Rensselaer Polytech,

Dartmouth and no other colleges. Both schools rejected me. For God's sake, the Dean at RPI was dad's close friend and a neighbor when I was growing up. Now my mom and dad were having serious concerns about my educational future. Growing up in Pittsfield, I often heard about Holy Cross College and the great sports programs they had. What the heck, this sounded like the perfect college for me. By the grace of God alone, a theme that would follow me for the rest of my life, the college accepted me in pre-med and psychology. Once again, God stepped in to help. He got me into a school that would provide a gateway towards a promising future, a future that I could never have predicted.

CHAPTER 4

MY EMERGENCE AS AN INDIVIDUAL WITH HOPES AND DREAMS

FRESHMAN AND SOPHOMORE YEARS

Holy Cross is a Jesuit College on one of Worcester, Massachusetts, seven hills. Established in 1843, the campus is beautiful, with many buildings dressed in ivy. During my four years, and yes, I graduated, there were about two-thousand students, or five- hundred in each class. I feel lucky to have gotten into this selective college. I was one of many students who, for the first time, faced the prospect of being alone and dependent on our abilities to fit in. Small classes and brilliant professors made this journey a fantastic experience.

If you are now lulled into thinking my education was a walk in the park, you are wrong. The challenges of college life, good, bad and indifferent, may surprise you.

I chose Holy Cross for several reasons. Primarily because I was accepted. Second, because the school had a golf team and a history of standout players. The third, short-lived reason, is that my high school girlfriend was attending Smith College, about a one-hour drive by car. Unfortunately, dad would not buy me an automobile during my freshman year. Man, was my dad a smart guy! I had to hitchhike for my visits.

During my first weekend at Holy Cross, our freshman class traveled on an introductory road trip to Falmouth, Massachusetts, on Cape Cod. Being from Albany, New York, I asked my new friends what was so special about "Fallmouth". In Massachusetts talk, the city was pronounced "Falmith". My error stayed with me for four years. What a way to start my college experience.

I was one of three freshmen who came to Holy Cross and made the starting roster on the golf team.

Throughout our four years on the team, Chuck Harty, Frank Levy and I rarely associated socially. We practiced golf together and played matches and tournaments as a team. We spent more time together than many students, not part of an athletic team. Our friendships would last for many years beyond graduation. Chuck and Frank were good people, a common thread amongst golfers.

My mother wanted me to be a doctor, so I was in the pre-med program. My other major was psychology. By the time my junior year came, I was no longer enrolled to be a doctor. Good news for me and many potential patients. The biology and chemistry classes and labs, and cell biology outpaced my intellect. At least I knew this before I wasted four years of tuition. Once I unloaded those science classes, and began taking economics, logic and philosophy courses, my grades were much better, and I finally enjoyed learning to learn again. LaSalle did an exceptional job in preparing me for these four years of growth and maturity.

During my freshman year, I made friends, experimented with pot and some other unmentionable things, and then experienced real heartbreak. After re-breaking my leg years earlier, recovering in Pittsfield, one of my dad's employees brought his daughter, Karen, to my room, hoping we might become close friends. Karen's dad had suffered a mental breakdown at work and my dad, being the caring and sensitive manager that he was, and I would become, helped him through his career-ending illness with General Electric. Dad later transferred and promoted him to General Electric Silicones in Waterford, New York.

Jack Welch became President and CEO of General Electric. He transferred my dad to Chicago. Jack wanted dad out of the way and sent him to the GE Supply Division, a big-time loser at the time. Like always, dad turned the division around, then retired, sort of. More on this later. My dad drove me hard and, like many fathers of his generation, never expressed whatever pride he might feel with his son. This went on until dad was in his eighties when, during a lunch trip to Park City, Utah, he finally told me he was proud of my career, but he couldn't understand how I managed an advanced high-technology company called Thor Guard.

After my breakup with Karen, I was offered a part-time job by a Holy Cross golf supporter during the winter. Bob liked me and wanted to help me make some extra money off season. For several weeks, working two nights a week from 8 PM to 2 AM, I would be a striker on a liquor delivery truck for Bob's distribution company. My friend Bob owned that beer distribution company. I got paid in cash. A lot of cash!

One night, while returning from our shift, with a few beers under our belt, the local police pulled the truck over. The officer asked me my name and how old I was. Well, I was underage for delivering booze and working after 10 PM. Fortunately; he was a big Holy Cross golf fan and knew who I was. He let us go with the promise that I would no longer work this job. My driver was also pardoned. Although it was sad to lose a job that paid well and provided plenty of beer as a bonus, the money I saved got me through the rest of my freshman year.

Many younger people do not know who Jack Welch (CEO of General Electric) was. My mom hated him and wanted my dad to be far more aggressive in pursuing promotions with General Electric. That was never in my father's nature, and I am so grateful he never followed that path. Jack had a well-deserved nickname, Neutron Jack. The top ten percent of the company executives he liked were well rewarded. The bottom ten percent disappeared from the company. Everyone else was on their own fighting for survival. I never wanted to work in such an environment, so GE would never be my employer. I had my own big plans.

If you haven't guessed by now, my life's desire after college would be successfully competing on the PGA Tour. That was the unshakeable plan for my future!

LOVING THE NEW LIFE

During the Holy Cross years, I had three roommates. I can only remember the names of the two. Tim Demkin and I were roomies for the first two years at the Cross. His mom would send ducks from the duck farm they owned on Eastern Long Island (the ducks were dead and cleaned so we ate them). Bob Burlison roomed with me my senior year. Holy Cross went co-ed in 1972. By our senior year, our room was now co-ed. We saw little of one another as Bob studied and I was playing golf or teaching skiing at Wachusett Mountain at night during the winter.

Because of my golf schedule, my classes were from 8:30AM to 12:30PM on Mondays, Wednesdays and Fridays. Pre-Med labs were on Thursday afternoons. I studied hard enough to get by, but my heart was just not into classwork.

After leaving the pre-med study program, I found my educational calling. I loved psychology, and I found the course work interesting and challenging. I even added enough course work in economics to consider another major until I found out I would need to take an additional statistics course. It would have been my third and there was no way I was going to ruin my GPA with another. After all, why would I need statistics to play professional golf? NOT!

In 1971, Holy Cross joined the Yankee Conference for athletics. Fall golf was good for me and I won most of the matches I played. In those days, our matches were against other schools. We played individual matches and the team with the most victories won the overall competition.

We typically played match play, like the professionals do in the Ryder Cup, and I did very well in that format. You could take 100 strokes on a hole and still win the match, because the match was per hole, with no aggregate score. I could make some big numbers in those days! Everything was wonderful until January after I returned from Christmas break.

I got mononucleosis. Life became miserable. I had to stay away from people, had to attend church alone, and became a recluse. Every night after studying, I would go to our class center, the Hart Center, and lock myself in a room with a piano. I would play two to three hours straight. I could even play Tommy, by the Who, without music. I was almost a rock star, but no one knew it. For the next two years, I would occasionally play the piano for fashion shows on campus. Best seat in the house!

Finally, by spring, I was mostly healthy and played a full golf schedule. On our spring weekend, we had the Yankee Conference Championship at Pleasant Valley Country Club. The weather was cold and windy. I played well the first day and returned to campus and partied hard with my friends. The last round of the event was even colder than the previous day. Temperature in the forties, wind over twenty miles an hour, with drizzle and snow flurries. To my amazement, I shot a final round 69 and tied for first place. Our coaches, who were overly competitive, wanted the two players to take part in a sudden death playoff. It was dark and snowing. The two of us said no. That is why we ended up tied. We were happy with that result.

By the next day, the school knew I had won, and I became popular with quite a few classmates in all classes. Those friendships would endure for many years. I would be remiss if I did not mention that a LaSalle classmate, Mike Dunne, won the pole vault championship in the Yankee Conference that same year.

After I won the championship, I thought I was infallible. I had lost a match a month later, and the team lost as well. This was only the second or third time that year we lost. I got back to my dorm room, Lehy room 222, and lost it. I threw my clubs out the window in a fit of rage. My temper would be an issue for many years to come. Before my semester was over, my dad was transferred to Chicago with General

Electric. I was not going to Chicago, period. Aunt Ruth and Uncle Jim Maloy, a very loving and special couple, hosted me during that summer. I got a night job with the Grand Union grocery chain unloading bananas from the crates coming from South America. These crates were full of big, ugly spiders. To this very day, I hate spiders. I also continued to play on the weekly Eastern New York Golf Association events to stay tournament sharp. I continued to play well in these events.

JUNIOR AND SENIOR YEAR - MY DEVELOPMENT AS AN INDIVIDUAL

I was slow to develop my comfort without mom and dad around. My classmates and teachers helped me grow and explore my life as it was. Little did I realize my life and understanding of my strengths and weaknesses was about to take some major turns. Some good and some, well, less than desirable. I am certain my classmates and other students in college navigate around these changes better than I did. In retrospect, those changes in me resulted in my re-birth on a human level.

I would leave the pre-med program in my first semester of junior year. With fresh courses I liked, I also had professors who cared and reinvigorated my will to learn. My grades went up and life was good. Life was almost easy!

Everyone on the golf team improved over the previous summer, and the team remained strong. A six-foot-nine freshman from New Jersey, Jimmy Dee, became a teammate. Jimmy's golf prowess was amazing. His family, who we came to know well, was in the golf business. His dad even played on the PGA Tour. Jimmy also had a loving and caring mom.

They both played a role in his immediate acceptance by everyone. Jimmy also played varsity basketball. Jimmy could hit the golf ball out of sight. With Jimmy, the team also got a new captain, Bob Noto. Like Jimmy, Bob and I also became friends away from the golf course.

During our junior year Christmas break, I asked Bob to join me and the family at Bromley Mountain in Vermont. Bob wanted to learn to ski. As a Long Island beach lifeguard, he was strong and fearless. I tried to teach him how to control his speed on the mountain and he was successful...in his own way. On a lower trail, he discovered that the best way for him to stop was by running into a fence. He stopped quickly, but it was neither pleasant nor elegant. Bromley Mountain didn't seem to care!

Bob also had diabetes. At the rented ski house at Bromley, with the Grays, my parents' lifelong friends, they found his needles. My mom and dad were horrified because they suspected he was using illegal drugs. It was quite funny when I explained his condition. They were so relieved. Bob thought it was one of the funniest moments in his life. I agreed. That incident cemented our friendship for the rest of the year.

I needed a job. This boy needed some money. I got hired as a ski instructor at Wachusett Mountain. Bruce McDonald was the ski school director. I was, because of my previous experience, one of the more senior members of the school. Bruce, like Court McDermott at Bousquet, enjoyed teaching his instructors and helping us to improve our ski technique and teaching prowess. Bruce's approach to teaching and managing would later become my own.

I could have taught advanced classes. My choice, once again, was to teach beginners because I could quickly see improvements in their skiing, and they wanted to learn. My methods were unorthodox, however. Normally, the instructors would place a student into a lower class if he or she was slow to advance their skiing skills.

Fortunately, I had the bottom class, so that option did not exist. The practice of moving better students into an advanced class or two resulted in the other students feeling like they were failing. Instead, I had the better skiers help me teach the less talented. By using this technique, everyone got better, faster. The student-teacher's helpers improved by teaching the same skills they had learned. This became another bedrock in my ability to communicate, have empathy for others, and believe everyone can learn to learn. Thank you, LaSalle, for instilling these traits at an earlier age. Until Thor Guard, this job was the best I ever had!

No love life? Not so fast. I met Diane, an incoming freshman. She was funny, pretty, and skied well. This relationship remained in place past my college graduation. She may never read this book, but I credit her with getting me through some difficult times, enabling me to remain centered as a caring human being. After I graduated, the distance and lack of time together pulled me away from her. Looking back, breaking up with her was not one of my better moments. She was a keeper!

The summer break between my Junior and senior years differed from the past summers. Mom and dad wanted me to come to Chicago and forgo another year in Albany playing golf. A job was waiting for me, as well as a second job. My parents' intent was to discourage me from pursuing a golf career. I did not compete in any tournaments that summer. Instead, I worked at a company called Lee Wards, an arts and crafts distributor. I took on the task of flow charting the operations of the warehouse. It was time consuming and often tedious, but I did well. I also worked as a busboy at a local high-end restaurant, the Barn of Barrington, where I met Arnold Palmer. He was playing in the Western Open. Arnold was so kind and relaxed. He even took the time to hear about my golf experiences. I will never forget that evening.

In the evenings after work, I would go to a local golf course, Thunderbird, to hit balls and occasionally play. I met the golf professional, Walt Wynarczyk, and his lovely wife Diane. Walt and I would practice together, and when the sun allowed, we would play a few holes before dark. He was an accomplished player, and we had some good matches. Fortunately, I also learned that when you meet someone you like, it is important to stay in touch. I kept up with Walt over the years after college. Walt would become one of my best friends, an employee and Thor Guard's most successful representative. More on Walt in a later chapter.

After this summer of hell, I was eager to return to Holy Cross for one last year. Wow, what an exceptional year it was! My golf game improved. I taught skiing for another season and started a ski acrobatic program. I directed this new class, because it was my idea. Classwork was fun and my grades reflected my love of learning. I also spent fall and spring weekends driving to Point Judith and Beavertail, Rhode Island, to fish for bluefish and stripers. The love of being near the water and fishing had become more ingrained in my existence than ever before.

One fall weekend I drove to Point Judith for an all-night fishing adventure for striped bass and bluefish. This was a surf fishing adventure, but there were no fish running that night. I remained there, hoping for some fish until around noon the next day. By the time I drove back to school, I was exhausted. Halfway to school, I fell asleep at the wheel and drove into the median separating the north and south freeways. My front wheel hit a drainage structure and immediately woke me up. I made my way back to the highway and pulled off at the next exit to see what damage I had done to the car. I pulled into a Dunkin' Donuts parking lot and checked. Thank God, there was no damage. To this point in my life, I never drank coffee. Needing something to wake up my tired brain, I ordered a large coffee. I made it back to my dorm room in one piece. To this very day, I have become used to my guardian angels helping me avoid death. Also, to this very day, I always drink Dunkin' Donuts coffee!

Our golf team, led by our coach Gerry Andersen, had blossomed into a powerful team in New England. Coach Andersen, Gerry, always wanted to have a team under his leadership compete in the NCAA championships. All we needed was to play in the New England championship, do well, and we would get an invitation. Father Brooks, the top dog at Holy Cross, would not let us compete because some of us had final exams that week. Even though our professors argued for us, Fr. Brooks would not change his mind. After four years of bringing Holy Cross to the forefront of college golf, it did not matter.

Gerry was a skilled player in his own right. Even at sixty-seven years old or so, he could still beat any of us. Perhaps the greatest putter I had ever seen. Julius Boros agreed Gerry was the best putter with whom he ever played. That was saying a lot. Gerry was our dear friend and as fine a coach as anyone could ever hope to have. Thank you, Gerry, for those exceptional years and life lessons you shared with the team.

In a previous chapter, I had mentioned how one teacher emerged as my favorite. Similarly, at Holy Cross, there was one unlikely recipient of this award. Dr. Ogretta McNeil was head of the psychology department and my student advisor. Her students referred to her affectionately as "Regretta". She was a gracious lady and a demanding teacher. She wanted her students to achieve perfection, at least in her eyes. I would often write a paper three or four times, at her direction, before she would grade my masterpiece. I seldom made her happy and got B's, not A's. Her demands on me as a student would become another tool in my professional life. Looking back, it is easy to respect and understand her efforts to help me become a successful individual.

Well, I graduated on time. I thought of it as a miracle, but really, I did the work and was ready to move forward with my life. Now, as I had been dreaming for years, it was time to leave this protected environment and become part of the real world. Never could I have realized that life was about to get difficult, often very difficult. The last evening that I was on campus before heading to Chicago, I went to the hillside parking area to look, for a last time, at the beautiful mountains surrounding Worcester.

Whenever I felt depressed or down, I would frequently visit this spot. It always helped. This time it brought great sadness to me because I realized that this old friend would never be there for me again.

Sadly, I drove away for the last time as a student but with great anticipation for what lie ahead. My dreams and life plans were soon to be put to the ultimate test. The life I dreamed of would be nothing I could ever have expected!

Foot Note: Mononucleosis is a contagious virus caught through transferring saliva. It attacks younger people, producing fatigue, fever, headaches and sore throats.

Foot Note: Thor Guard manufactures Lightning Prediction and Warning System in Sunrise, Florida.

CHAPTER 5

AN UNEASY PATH
FORWARD

After graduation, I started my new life at home in Barrington, Illinois, with my parents. This was supposed to be a time of reflection, preparation for my PGA Tour qualifying, and taking a part-time job for pocket money. My world would come crashing down soon after my arrival at home.

My dad and I would play golf together. Because his handicap was above twenty, and mine was between +2 and +5, our matches were not close. I would sometimes borrow a set of left-handed clubs and play without giving him any strokes. The competition was far more equitable because I could not play well from the right side of a golf ball. This round of golf would be different.

We went to Lake Geneva, Wisconsin, to play the Jack Nicklaus designed Briar Patch at the old Playboy Club. This course was long, hilly and very difficult. I played right-handed, my normal side of the ball. The round started out like usual, but dad could not play this course well. That day I played exceptionally well, firing a sixty-nine, three under par. I was proud of my round and glad dad could see a great round of golf. On the way home, the conversation got around to what I was going to do for a living. I was driving. I informed him I would join the PGA Tour and live my life as a professional golfer. To my amazement and chagrin, he told me to forget those dreams because I was not good enough. I managed to control my temper until I got home. Once home, I went to my room and, with my usual temper, I destroyed every trophy I had garnered over the years. The only two that survived were a little league all-star trophy, and the trophy I had won at LaSalle for the Catholic league championship. I also got mad at God for this devastating disruption of my dreams. From now on in my life, I would often blame God for my failures, then apologize to Him for getting mad. As mentioned earlier, this back and forth with God would last for many years.

Early that summer, my neighbor from Lee Wards offered me a full-time job. I respectfully turned the position down because dad thought I should accept the offer. That was my revenge. I spent most of that summer looking for a job and honing my golf skills for my future in golf. I spent time playing golf at Crystal Lake Country Club in Illinois and with Walt at Thunderbird. Finally, I had control of my life, and I was happy. Dad's relationship with me got better but would never be close again!

My job search found a position away from home in the fall of 1975. I joined Cerro Metals in Bellefonte, Pennsylvania, as a trainee for a sales position. I moved to State College for the winter and worked under Charlie Dolan. He was a great supervisor, managed like dad, and played golf well. We became fast friends. Besides learning the brass rod, forging and casting business, I also volunteered to do another massive flow chart for the plant's operations. I guess I enjoyed talking to the workers and getting an understanding of the problems encountered every day. In the beginning, the employees thought I was critiquing their jobs for expulsion. However, because I was such a nice guy, they came to understand that I was helping to make their jobs more efficient. Eventually, I had many friends throughout the company. It appeared the president liked me as well.

That summer, I met my future wife, Nancy. I would frequently drive from State College, Pennsylvania, non-stop overnight, to visit her in Chicago. Eight- hours of driving for these brief visits. It was worth it for my childish heart! The following year, I was transferred to St. Louis for further training in the field. My trainer was Tom, an elderly salesman. I learned so much from him while living in a rented room with other people. That experience royally sucked. What I learned from Tom was that the most important aspects of being successful were honesty and relationship building. His customers liked Tom, and we would meet with them just to chat. Sales would come from those personal relationships. I would follow those virtues for the rest of my life.

After training, I was promoted to Chicago to work for another seasoned salesperson and golfer. Bill Grimm was good to me over those years representing Cerro Metals in northern Illinois, Wisconsin and Minnesota. That summer, I got married to Nancy and held our reception at the Barn of Barrington.

During the wedding ceremony, something from beyond provided a sign, but we didn't recognize it. There was a major car crash outside the church just before the "I do's" were pronounced. Foreboding a dark future ahead? Yes.

Nancy was a beautiful and nice lady. I was a handful as I worked long hours, then played golf to prepare for the Tour.

We tried to get along, but fighting became an everyday part of our life together. There was one blessing that came from our childless relationship. Our adopted dog, Elle. A flat-coated retrieved who loved us both, sang with me when I played the piano, and accompanied me on my nightly jogs. Later, when Elle died, I began to understand loss and sadness. Because of that loss, I would never again have a dog in my life.

BACK TO GOLF

The winter before my PGA Tour qualifying, I traveled to Marco Island, Florida, for a month of winter practice. Strange how the future holds many surprises as I now live on Marco Island. While there, as a Wilson Staff member, I met Ken Venturi and Gene Sarazen, both professionals at the Island Country Club. They were both Wilson Staff members as well. We became friends and drank quite a bit. Ken and I would be friends until his death on May 17, 2013. We would see one another at the Masters tournament during the four years I provided lightning and weather forecast services. Later, when I moved to Marco Island, we would see one another at restaurants, golf events and church. He was a giving and wonderful individual I will never regret meeting.

I needed to do something drastic about my volcanic temper. This temper would hurt me in anything I might pursue in the future, but at this time, golf was the intended target. In school, I took classes in abnormal psychology where we learned about hypnosis, subliminal suggestions, and the subconscious mind. I took what I had remembered and taught myself self-hypnosis. I could go deep during my self-imposed sessions and coupled those calm feelings of being under with simple breathing exercises. Whenever I was about to explode, I would move away from people around me and take nine breaths and find that sense of calm. It worked very well. In later years, I used this experience to create a subliminal golf cassette for golf. It was called Mind Power Golf. More on this later.

I qualified in the initial rounds of the PGA Tour qualifying and moved on to the second stage, seventy two holes in Gretna, LA. Now I found myself with the big boys. I hit the ball as well as anyone there, but in the end, I failed to move on to the finals. I did not make any putts in the fifteen to thirty-foot range. That was a serious shortfall that I would work on the following year. I was unable to improve after much practice. I quit trying out for the PGA Tour and got my amateur status back the following year. Another failure and a reason to blame God for my failure to achieve my life's dream. This time, the choice to quit was my own, not my dad's.

I played golf at Crystal Lake Country Club with everyone. One young man, Pat Corey, would play with me all the time. He would also be a caddy for me in the club championship. In a way, I was his golf mentor, and I treated him like he was my son. He saw my golf when I was good. In 1978, I broke the course record with sixty-three, a record that stood for over forty years. For several weeks after that glorious round, we would play after work. I continued playing well enough to break my record several times, but we always had to stop playing because of darkness. Pat would win the Illinois State High School championship. Long before Pat's win, his father, Mike, recruited me to join his executive search firm.

Mike always believed that talented athletes made good businessmen. I was an almost perfect fit. I learned about the recruiting business, recruiting actuaries and human resource consultants. Mike's wife, Cathy, was a gem. She loved the

Who so, to me, she was perfect. The experience with Mike's firm taught me how to read and write resumes, interview candidates, understand professional positions and the company philosophies for whom I was recruiting. It was a wonderful experience until Mike's partner, Larry, wanted me out. Mike did not step in and allowed me to go. Another failure and another opportunity to blame God for my misfortunes. I admit, I hated Mike for abandoning me. That all being said, if I had not been fired, the rest of my life would not have turned out like it did. God stepped in, but not in a way I could fully understand.

Now I found myself in trouble. What do I do? I am getting divorced; I have no job, and absolutely no idea where I was going. To me, this was a total collapse of my life. Around the same time, my dad took a job, after he retired from General Electric, with GTE in Salt Lake City, Utah. The story behind this relocation is interesting, to say the least.

When Jack Welch got the big job, several high-level executives left General Electric. One of these individuals was Tom Vanderslice, who later became Chairman of GTE in Connecticut. He and dad were good friends. Once, during my first summer in Chicago, Tom came to visit my dad at our house. We were all talking about golf when Tom asked me if I wanted to attend the Masters Golf Tournament with him and my dad. Being the idiot I was, I told Tom that I would go to the Masters only when I received an invitation. He looked at me in amazement and proclaimed that I was the total loss from Holy Cross. As a Boston College graduate, this was funny. Later, I discovered Tom wintered in Naples, Florida, and I invited him to breakfast. We had a delightful time, mostly talking about my dad who had recently passed away. Tom reminded me of that afternoon's conversation, and I explained to him I got an invitation to the Masters

Tournament, but as a weather and lightning consultant, for four years. We both got a good laugh over that!

Back to my work despair. I eventually worked with a wonderful man named Bob Wolfson, who had a small search firm. Another recruiter from Mike's firm, Brett Lichty, joined us. This job lasted less than two years, but the experience was invaluable.

One winter day, Bob and I went to New York city, to sell our services to an insurance firm. I drove from Chicago to New York City in my new Porsche. In Indiana, during heavy snow, I dozed off and off the road we went. We hit a pole that destroyed the side mirror, broke the window and damaged the right side of the car. Like in Planes, Trains and Automobiles, we forged ahead because the car was drivable, and the radio worked. We were freezing but made it to our destination. We successfully landed the contract, then had another chilly drive back during the day! That was as much fun as I could stand.

I ended up leaving Bob's company, deciding to start my own consulting firm, R.M. Dugan and Associates. This was to be a major change to my life and a challenge for survival. I would be all alone, trying to make a living with no backstop.

CHAPTER 6

UNSPOKEN GUIDANCE FROM ABOVE

The world around me was changing. I seldom spoke in mean words to Jesus, but I spent more time thanking Him for my newfound success. This was a welcome change and probably opened the door for many of the extraordinary events to follow. For the first time in my life, I realized God was there to help me achieve the goals He had for me. Nothing could ever have prepared me for the life I would have over the next eight years and the following thirty years.

My consulting career was finally successful. I was financially well off and on my own for the first time in my life. This was a great feeling and a time for celebration and creativity. I soon discovered that I did not like recruiting, but I forged ahead because the money was so good. I became friends with many of my clients and nurtured them, using the training I had received at Cerro Metals years earlier. Even with my heavy workload, I still had time for new ventures.

Self-hypnosis had helped control my temper tantrums. I believed it was time to take that experience and help golfers improve their games. I researched subliminal messaging and created the first subliminal golf improvement tape. Using the color scheme of the Masters, I created the artwork for the tape and hired a professional studio to create the product. A dear friend, Judy Ressler, helped me with the artwork and production. The tape contained twenty positive messages, recorded beneath the sound of waves and seagulls. The sounds were soothing and opened the subconscious mind to the positive messages buried beneath. In a normal listening session of half an hour, the subconscious mind would understand these positive, soothing messages repeated over one thousand times. The tape was successful and helped the thousands of golfers who purchased Mind Power Golf. Charlie Stine, publisher of Golf Week magazine, purchased one for testing. He wrote a wonderful article reviewing the tape. Charlie had one caveat for his readers. He did not improve on the golf course, but his wife would listen at bedtime and readily fall asleep. Perfect!

My golf game was still competitive, but my left leg was getting weaker. This was a symptom called post-polio syndrome and happened to everyone afflicted by this horrible disease. This weakness would force me to discontinue my annual attempts to qualify for the USGA Open. In those days, qualifying was thirty-six holes in one day and you had to walk. I was too cheap to hire a caddy, so I carried my bag as well.

My last attempt to qualify was at Medinah Country Club in Illinois, where I played with a skilled player and friend Dino Lucchesi. After falling twice on a short, uphill par three, I was ready to quit. Dino would not let me quit, so I limped through the thirty-six holes. That day, I made a parting hole-in-one, one of nine in my life. The perfect ending to what I thought would be my lifelong pursuit of golf. Failure? Not this time. Nature decided for me.

During this same time in my life, I won twice with different partners, the highly acclaimed Butler Invitational in Oak Brook, Illinois. The course was tough but seemed to fit my game. The third year I played with another friend, and we finished second. After this event, I knew the game was slipping away, and I never played in the event again.

I previously mentioned that recruiting no longer satisfied my career objectives. One of my clients, the world's largest insurance brokerage firm with a large management consulting practice, hired me to develop an internal recruiting program to lessen the need for companies with my services. I spent a year on this project reporting to the president, and it was a near-total success. Why do I say near total? My last recruiting engagement with them was also the highest profile position for which I had ever been retained. I found the perfect consulting actuary and all he wanted was to sit down with the president to understand his vision for the company. In my report, I clarified that for recruits at this level, a meeting with the president was mandatory.

The president's refusal to meet with my talented candidate and his pulling out of negotiations resulted in me losing a tremendous bonus. For me, this would lead to the end of my recruiting days. After this, I took on fewer jobs then met a new friend and client, Bob Pugh. I would work for and with Bob for several years. Our friendship survived until his death several years ago. As I have become older, I grieve for fallen friends too frequently.

CHAPTER 7

FRIENDS, MORE FRIENDS AND THE TRIP OF A LIFETIME

L ife was good, but I was ready for a change in my career again. This time, a change would not be someone else's act, but one of my own. The problem was that I did not know what I would do at this point with my life.

I wanted to continue working in my company, but the future was empty, not one with plans or a target industry. After all my moves over the years, I knew something worthwhile would emerge that would satisfy my desires. I never dreamed or imagined the changes that were in store for me.

God would save me again in a profound and disguised manner. This time around, I was not in fear of failure. I was now convinced that whatever road I followed, I would be successful. It was an overwhelming sense of confidence that I embraced.

New friends that came into my life blessed these years. Joe was one. We met at a local bar owned by the great Walter Payton of Chicago Bears fame. Studebakers, in Schaumburg, Illinois, would become my second home. Joe and I met there and became lifelong friends. He introduced me to his high school golf buddies. At the end of every summer, we would play in the Six-Pack Open. Two days of playing golf and partying. Also, Joe introduced me to Jimmy and Tom. Times were great and these friendships would endure.

After my divorce, I dated many great women. I would see someone for a while, always looking for some flaw that I couldn't live with. I always found an issue and would break off the relationship so I could resume my search for a better lover. Admittedly, I was not a nice person during this time. I was often without compassion. Clearly, I just wanted to get on with another relationship, always seeking perfection I had not yet found. I am not proud of those days, eventually deciding there was no one in the world for me to love forever. This was a sobering realization that was, as you will discover later, entirely wrong. She existed, but I had not yet found her!

Remember Mike, my former boss? One day in 1986, he called me out of the blue and asked me to join two of his friends for a fishing trip to Costa Rica. I was still mad at Mike after all these years for what I perceived as his abandonment of me, and I had no interest in going anywhere with him. Somewhere deep in my subconscious, against all my logical misgivings, I went. This trip became another turning point in my life. What are the odds?

The trip took us to San Jose, Costa Rica, where we spent the night partying, then to the coastal waters of the Caribbean jungle. On the quick plane ride, the left engine warning light came on and we all thought this was the end. Our pilot didn't seem to care! The plane landed safely on the beach with the warning light still flashing.

The camp, Parismina Tarpon Rancho, was isolated on the edge of the jungle. These cabins were raised five to six feet above the ground to ensure that wild creatures could not eat the guests. Each morning, we would get up, have breakfast and head out fishing. The fishing for tarpon and snook was fantastic. Around noon, we would come back to the lodge for lunch, take a short siesta, and back out fishing until 4 PM. We would have fresh fish and fruit for dinner, then back to our rooms for the evening. There was no leaving the protective walls of our rooms. The evenings were spent drinking and having guests visit their new neighbors. One evening, while we were all sitting around discussing the day's fishing challenges, a tall lanky guy enters our room to visit. Bob, as we would call him, introduced himself as Robert Wood and joined in our lively discussion of the day. He published the Fishing Tackle Trade News and was writing a story about the camp. Bob talked about his professional background, and we did as well. He took our names and contact information and left. We never saw him again at the camp. This chance meeting and welcoming him into our temporary home would soon become an example of why you always treat people with respect and take an interest in their stories.

The rest of the trip went well. I was looking for some prank I could pull on Mike because I needed to get even for that fateful firing from my job many years earlier. This area had some deadly snakes, particularly the bushmaster. On the last day, we went to the beach to observe all the crosses placed in the water where sharks had eaten the natives. The path back to the main cabin was sandy, surrounded by dense brush. With Warren and Hammer behind me, I took a stick with two prongs and stuck it lightly into the back of Mike's leg. He thought a snake had bitten him! It was funny, but in hindsight, not a nice thing to do. Looking back on my prank, it was creative. Afterwards, Warren, Hammer, Mike and I returned home without incident.

When I got back to Chicago, I realized Mike did not cause my firing from his firm; it was all me. My mind was now at peace, and I would move forward forgiving others who I believe wronged me. Taking personal responsibility for my actions took many years to accept, but I was pleased I eventually got there.

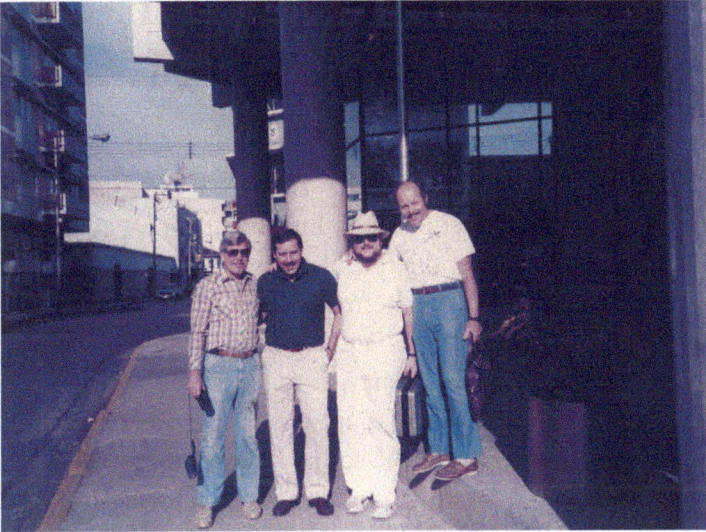

Boys in Costa Rica

CHAPTER 8

THE NORTHERN AMATEUR GOLF TOURNAMENT

During the winter of 1987, I read that a local golf event, run by my friend Ace Ellis, was being played at Sand Creek Country Club in Chesterton, Indiana. The course was owned by Bethlehem Steel and was comparable to Augusta National. I entered the event just to have the chance to play this gem. Even though my tournament days were over, I did not care. This was about the course - not victory.

I was not expecting anything good to come from my play, but as I was preparing to putt for another birdie on the eighth hole to go five-under par, lightning struck close by. Lightning was too close to continue to play. No lightning alert horns sounded suspending play, so I informed my competitors that I was going to the clubhouse. Ace Ellis, the tournament director, did not like our decision, but the rules of golf gave us that option, and it was the right decision because the storm was dangerous. After the tournament concluded and I secured a second-place finish, I expressed my dissatisfaction with the organization of the event. Ace told me that if I thought I could do a better job running the event, I should take control of the Northern Amateur in the future. I readily accepted the role.

This became another decision that would again alter the entire trajectory of my life.

Coincidentally, that same year, I received a call from Robert Wood, the gentleman I met in Costa Rica. He told me he recently sold the publication and was working with an inventor in Doral, Florida, who had created a unique fish finder. Rather than a downward-looking sonar, it acted like a scanning underwater radar. The device was called Sona Scan. It was an exceptional device I successfully used in Lake Michigan when trolling for Skamania Steelhead, and on trips to Wisconsin, casting for muskie, the fish of ten thousand-casts. On Lake Michigan, I could scan the top ten feet of the water column and locate the steelhead, sometimes eighty feet from both sides of the boat. For the muskie, we could scan an entire shoreline from one location and see the muskie or pike staging to attack their next lunch. The inventor, Bob Humphreys, had created a useful tool I added to my fishing hardware. This was brilliant technology!

These seemingly unconnected events would change my life, and the lives of many other people I had not yet met, forever.

Me at the 1989 Northern Amateur

CHAPTER 9

MY LOVE OF FISHING AND BOATS

Along with golf, fishing was a great joy in my life. Even though I enjoyed fly-fishing in rivers wearing waders or going on charter boats in Lake Michigan trolling for salmon and trout, I needed a boat. I started out with a Bomber outboard that was not an efficient fishing platform. I sold it and purchased a Tuffy walleye and muskie open fisherman. This was a fantastic boat but too dangerous for fishing in Lake Michigan. I did not want to sell the Tuffy, so I added a twenty-one-foot Pursuit cuddy cabin to fish the enormous lake. Powered by a 200 horsepower Yamaha outboard motor, I could get out to the fish, troll all day, and get home safely. I could cross the lake to the state of Michigan and did so many times. This trip was about eighty miles. But after getting caught in a few nasty storms, the Pursuit had to go.

The Tuffy was a great boat. On my trips to Marco Island during Christmas to visit my folks who were vacationing there, I would trailer the Tuffy from Chicago for my fishing exploration of the Everglades. This boat was the perfect boat for fishing in these shallow waters. I would catch trout, snook, sheepshead and tarpon at will. Anglers in Marco had never seen this boat, and it became a relative hit as a fishing platform. I came to love these waters and the mangrove-lined shorelines. Once again, little did I know Marco Island would later become my home.

An enormous Wellcraft 3300 Coastal replaced the Pursuit. Loaded with electric downriggers and an outstanding Furuno sonar, this boat became a well-known sight on the lake. It could handle all weather and travel as far as I wanted in safety and comfort. Aptly named Head Hunter, she was almost perfect. During my second winter layover, a significant crack developed along the keel. Fortunately, the boat was under warranty and Wellcraft took the boat back to Sarasota, Florida, for a new hull. The people working on the boat were fantastic and did not mind my visits to oversee their efforts. I asked them to install a conduit for my downrigger power cables and to provide a hardtop to keep me dry on bad days. They did all that and added an overhead compartment for my Furuno fish finder. Now I had the perfect boat, but she needed a new name. The salmon slayer was now called Head Hunter II. More on this gem later!

To control the explosive alewife population, salmon were introduced into the Great Lakes. Alewives are a breed of herring. Their death after spawning would stink up the beaches. The newly introduced king and coho salmon would feed on the abundance of these baitfish and grow quickly to enormous sizes. Later, two species of steelhead would be introduced into Lake Michigan. The native trout, perch and northern pike populations would also grow. Largemouth and smallmouth bass were already plentiful, especially in Green Bay and the waters of Door County, Wisconsin. Door County would become the favorite summer destination for Susan and me. More on this later!

Head Hunter II

CHAPTER 10

MUSIC AND AUDIO TECHNOLOGY IN MY LIFE

I have always loved music and the sounds of musical instruments and female vocalists. My musical tastes widely varied from hard rock, soft rock, country rock, female vocals to some classical music. I wasn't a big fan of Broadway musicals until I listened to music written by Andrew Lloyd Weber. I loved most of his compositions, especially Phantom of the Opera and Evita.

In the early days of my music listening experience, I listened to cassettes and vinyl. I met some of the finest designers and manufacturers of audio equipment, like Bill Conrad and Lew Johnson of Conrad Johnson, Bill Johnson of Audio Research fame, the owner of Karsten Custom Speakers, and Geoff Poor of Balanced Audio Technologies. I studied circuit board designs and learned about the different technologies, including tubes, Class A amplification, Class AB amplification, reel-to-reel recording practices, and finally digital technology used in CD players and amplifiers.

I am not an engineer, so many of the papers I read went way over my head. It did not matter. I enjoyed learning what I could, talking to the designers and engineers who had created this wonderful way to listen to recorded music. After many years of trial and error, and money, I assembled a collection of audio equipment that would fulfill my demands for quality music reproduction in my home. In college, I began purchasing records and kept them all. Today, I am blessed with over 200 records I enjoy. To my amazement, there are no scratches that would have destroyed these gems of my past.

My favorite performers included, but not limited to, were The Beatles, Beach Boys, Vanilla Fudge, Bread, the Bee Gees, the Classics IV, The Who, The Eagles, America, Rita Coolidge, my favorite female vocalist Karen Carpenter, Journey, Pink Floyd, Stevie Nicks, Led Zeppelin, Donovan, John Denver, The Supremes, The Moody Blues, Kenny Rogers, Bob Dylan, Olivia Newton John, Dan Fogelberg, Alan Parsons, Crosby, Stills, Nash and Young, Chicago, Celene Dion and many others. Each group or performer fulfilled some deep-seated need, fitting into the fabric of my life.

My interest in the individual parts and components placed onto circuit boards would help me in my future role with Thor Guard. This was another example of how curiosity about life and integrating seemingly unrelated interests of your past can become relevant in the future. My folks would often tell me I had too many distractions in my life to be successful. I prefer to say that I was insatiably curious, but either way, I am so happy that I was distracted!

PART TWO

CHAPTER 11

THE LAST NORMAL YEAR OF MY LIFE

1988 was the first year I would be the director of the Northern Amateur Golf Tournament. I was driven to make this tournament a nationally recognized premier event.

I continued to consult in my recruiting business and spent time in meetings with Sand Creek members and the General Manager, Kevin Smith, so that everything would proceed as planned. The membership was committed to making this a special event. I convinced a friend, John Watson, who managed the Jaymar Ruby clothing store in Schaumburg, Illinois, to have his company, Jaymar, partially sponsor our event. Remember Gary Adams? I spoke with him and Taylor Made also became a major sponsor of The Northern Amateur. We offered breakfast, lunch, and dinner during each of the tournament rounds. We meticulously laid out everything on paper. The event went exactly as we had hoped for. Fortunately, the weather was never dangerous and did not disrupt play. By the next year, The Northern Amateur was a top ten amateur event in the United States of America.

That fall, I received another call from Robert Wood. He told me the inventor of my great fish finder also had invented a lightning prediction system. I shared my belief that lightning couldn't be predicted and ended the conversation. He also asked me if I would be interested in working with his good friend, Gary Loomis, owner of G. Loomis fishing, to help him design and build golf shafts. Gary's company manufactured the finest graphite fishing rods in the world, and his CFO, John, wanted to make golf shafts. John did not fish so Gary, to make John happy, agreed to go into a new market of which Gary knew nothing. I was all in with one stipulation: Gary could not pay me with money, but he could reimburse my efforts with fishing rods. I had enough money but could never have enough great fishing rods. That fall, we began our journey together.

Gary was an amazing individual who knew more about tubular graphite construction than anyone alive. This technology was ahead of its time and would revolutionize both professional and amateur golf for many years. Gary was someone I immediately admired and liked. I visited his group of trailers where he made his magic happen. Woodland, Washington, was a damp, cold and uncomfortable place surrounded by beautiful mountains, if you could see them. The grounds around his trailers were muddy and dirty. Inside his manufacturing facility was a totally different story. Cleanly organized and full of artisans who were expert craftsmen. I was not aware yet, but the machinery used to roll the fishing rods was unique and designed by his son, Brad. I will not get into the machinery with respect to the company's secrets. However, they could compress the layers of graphite up to 350 pounds per square inch, compared to traditional manufacturing methods, still used today, that could only achieve 35 to 50 pounds per square inch.

He could use wild custom mandrels used to form the rods with tapers only his technology could produce. What this meant was that less resin was used to make the rod. More of graphite's strengths were utilized to produce rods with the exact properties required for different uses. I was like a sieve. After some thought, I realized he could build an iron shaft better than any shaft of any material ever produced.

After over two years of designing and testing, we had it. We could totally control the flex points of every shaft, produce shafts with torque less than steel, and deliver to the consumer a shaft that would help any golfer hit the ball farther and straighter while still feeling good. The shafts were a hit on the PGA Tour and won a United States Open Championship in Michigan. To this very day, Gary is one of many individuals I totally respect and like as a friend. Remember those fishing rods for which I traded my efforts? I received plenty and have used them lovingly ever since. As with the golf shafts, G. Loomis rods are the best I have ever used!

CHAPTER 12

DID THIS REALLY HAPPEN?

1989 was shaping up to be a fantastic year. I had finally overcome my menacing temper. Business was good and my love life was normally abnormal. I was working hard on my recruiting business. I went to the gym regularly, and each day was completely full. My evenings at Studebakers continued to be a blast with free food and plenty of drinking.

Gary Loomis and his nephew, Bobby Loomis, were becoming my good friends. When we were not working on the golf shafts, we were discussing all aspects of fishing. Bobby and Gary were true outdoorsmen and accomplished hunters and anglers. I learned a great deal from each one. Our conversations included fishing rod and golf shaft design, and many aspects of lure presentations. I could never have chosen better teachers. This work was fun!

I spent many vacations visiting my parents in Salt Lake City. Well, I visited them and skied some enormous mountains, blessed with the greatest snow on earth. Everything was just right.

The Northern Amateur was to be held in August. All the volunteers and staff members were well trained and after many meetings prior to the event, the tournament would be nothing short of perfect. That is what I had planned. I still had one lingering problem. Robert Wood was really pushing me to have Bob Humphreys bring his Thor Guard lightning prediction device to the tournament. I did everything I could do, with enormous respect, to say I was not interested in having an untested device at my precious golf event. Fortunately, something in my brain pushed me to indulge this man. At the very least, I could sit down with Bob and thank him for his wonderful fish finder. No harm, no foul!

I would always check the weather before each round of my tournament so that I had some idea what to expect from mother nature. The forecast for our tournament was good. No concerns. I would play my first round in the morning, have lunch, then meet with Kevin Smith to discuss next year's event, and the cost to The Northern Amateur for the following year. We always enjoyed these leisurely hours, enjoying some scotch to make negotiations more pleasant. I was not prepared for the events that followed. There would be another event that would change my life forever.

I did not play particularly well on this beautiful Thursday morning. The day was in the eighties, not much wind and cloudless. I had lunch and went to Kevin's office for our ritual. At around 3 PM, Bob Humphreys radioed us requesting that we suspend play because of lightning. Kevin and I laughed and walked out to his office patio and looked up at the clear blue skies. Bob was an inventor and a genuine character. Kevin and I disregarded the warning based on our own observations of a blue, virtually cloudless sky. However, two minutes later, Bob contacted us again in a panic, stressing the urgency of clearing the golf course. Against my better judgement, I succumbed to the pressure and sent the message to the volunteers that the play was suspended, and everyone should return to the clubhouse or seek shelter on the course. Everyone believed this was crazy and with not a cloud in the sky, so there was no mad rush back to seek shelter. Our decision confused everyone, me included.

Kevin and I were now back to negotiating and shaking our heads at our baseless decision. Roughly eleven minutes after Bob had first asked us to suspend the tournament, we heard and felt a massive thunderclap that shook the clubhouse. At first, we couldn't believe our lying ears, then the truth of what occurred sunk in. Unfortunately, because the players and volunteers were in no hurry to seek shelter, six players were indirectly struck by that massive lightning strike on the eighteenth hole. We later learned that a storm had created what is referred to in meteorology as a "Bolt Out of the Blue". This strike came from a massive storm over Waukegan, Illinois, over fifty miles away from the golf course. My perfect tournament was no longer so perfect!

The club called an ambulance for assistance, but fortunately, none of the players were injured, just badly shaken. What a combination, a strange lightning strike and, miraculously, no serious injuries. As if this disaster was not enough, I now had an additional issue with which to contend.

This golf tournament was open to players of any age, with handicaps of ten or less. We had competitors from their early teens to competitors in their fifties. While we were waiting for more lightning to bombard us, we learned a teenager had broken the course record earlier in the day. After a fifteen-minute wait, Bob informed us that the lightning was over for now and we could resume play.

Not so fast! A few parents who were there with their kids did not want them to go back out and play on this lightning-prone piece of Indiana property. We had to resume play or cancel the tournament and negate the young man's course record. As if seeing Bob's lightning predictor work wasn't enough, I now had to decide the future of the 1989 Northern Amateur. I began questioning the logic of becoming the director of this tournament. It was time to call the United States Golf Association for advice.

I reached a golf rules official at the USGA's headquarters in Far Hills, New Jersey. I began speaking with Tony Zirpoli about my event. I told him we had more than half of the field finished with their rounds, but a few parents would not allow them back to play because of the strange lightning strike we predicted. Tony then asked, "Do you have a lightning predictor?" Again, I said yes, then asked what I needed to do to get my tournament finished. He again asked about the device that predicted the lightning strike. Eventually, he suggested disqualifying any players who did not wish to resume play, but only if I was assured that it was safe to resume play. Luckily, the kids continued to play, and fortunately, there were no more lightning strikes for the rest of Thursday or Friday.

Kevin and I went back to his office to continue our negotiations. At first, we sat silently, looking at one another. Kevin knew I was thinking about changing careers and knew I did not know what job I wanted. He then looked at me and said, and I quote, "God just spoke to you and told you what your new job would be". At this time, I did not know what job to which he was referring. Years later, this day represented just another significant event in my life's journey.

The Northern Amateur would finish in 1989 with no more surprises. What a strange way to find a new job!

You might ask yourself if this was the most significant event in my changing life? The answer is no! You can put that thought to rest. There are many more yet to come!

CHAPTER 13

MORE CHALLENGES
AND CELEBRATIONS

Converging thoughts of success and failures from 1989 filled my head. I witnessed a rare lightning strike prediction where, miraculously, no one suffered serious injuries. I originally felt that I had failed the competitors, not warning them of an incoming lightning strike in a timely manner.

As the year ended, I was no closer to finding a new career. My love life was in tatters, and I had no expectations for any revelations coming soon. I was not overly concerned about my future because I knew something special was on the horizon. I did not know that another significant event in my life was about to frame my future.

My days were always busy, typically working from 8 AM to 6 PM. Mind Power Golf had become too much for me to handle, so I would close the doors to the business by mid-summer. My search business was going well, even though my enthusiasm was less than I would have liked. G. Loomis was progressing well. And as in the past, I would spend every evening at Studebakers, enjoying free food and plenty of booze. While this lifestyle was getting old, I enjoyed catching up on the latest news with my friends. To me, Studebakers was my "Cheers" place to live. The parallels between the two are uncanny in terms of characters and nightly experiences. Studebakers had become my second home, although I was not proud of that. It was just a fun place to go to forget my woes!

Walter Payton was frequently in his office behind the bar. He did not come out of his office too often but was hands on running the place. On one fateful evening, I was having a drink when Duke, a good friend and bartender, handed me a questionnaire to complete. I asked him what it was for, but he just said Walter wanted me to complete it. There were some interesting questions pertaining to my life, what I enjoyed, my work, and what the last book I read was. I honestly answered the questions as best as I could. The last book-read question was interesting. I had recently done some work on my boat engines, so I purchased and read the Mercruiser Maintenance Manual cover to cover. That was the last book I read, so that was my answer. I gave the questionnaire back to Duke and forgot about it. I never even thought about its purpose.

In early spring, I received a call from a marketing firm. The representative was very nice and informed me I was a finalist in the contest for a normal, non-celebrity representative for Dewar's Scotch. She also asked me to change the last book read to something more sophisticated. I chose "Barbarians at the Gate", a book choice that seemed to please her. I then asked her who the other finalists were. There were two others, and I knew one of them. That finalist had worked with me at Mike Corey's firm. At that point, I knew I was to be eliminated because he had been a crew member on the Stars of America race boat and had competed in the

America's Cup. A month later, I would find out how wrong I was. I was now Dewar's scotch Do-Er profile personality! It blew me away.

When my father discovered the" honor" his son had received, it horrified him. On the one hand, his son was now representing a famous alcohol brand, and because I drank scotch. On the other hand, it was not the brand he drank, J&B. I tried explaining to him it was just a contest and had absolutely nothing to do with my drinking habits. Regardless of his disappointment, I felt elated and strangely popular with my Studebaker friends.

Little did I know this award would lead to a story in the Chicago Tribune. Once again, I am reminded that strange things were affecting my life.

The rest of the year was a blur. Perhaps one reason was that I was drinking six to eight scotches five nights a week. I knew it was bad for me, but I did not want to stop. Strangely, it got to where all those drinks did not affect me negatively. Aside from those minor concerns, business was substantial, my friend base was growing, and I was even playing more golf. Golf had become fun again, and I seldom got mad when I hit a wayward shot. Mind Power Golf was working for me.

You may wonder if the love of my life had somehow miraculously descended into my life? The short and only answer is no! Fortunately, my search for my soulmate had taken a back seat to everything else going on in my life. I was just too critical of any woman because I wanted perfect love, a love for the ages, I guess. I was thirty seven years old and figured I still had time. I was not interested in having children, so all was well.

Foot Note: Mercruiser is an inboard boat motor manufactured by Mercury Marine.

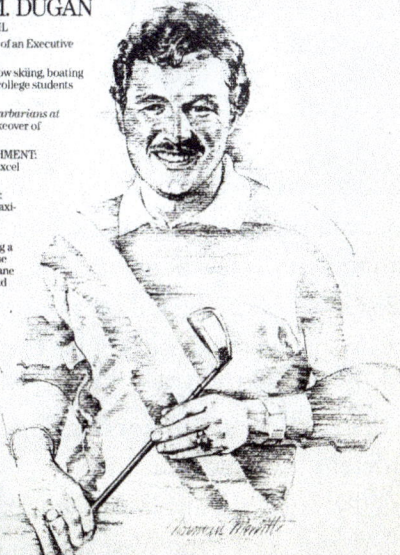

My Dewar's Do-Er ad

CHAPTER 14

SHIFTING SANDS, AND A NEW FRIEND

Winters in Chicago were never much fun. I would occasionally go to a small ski area on the border with Wisconsin to ski for a few hours with my friend Steve Furuta, just to keep my legs strong and break up winter's monotony. I had already planned to visit my parents in Salt Lake City during Christmas of 1990, so I needed to be in shape to ski safely on these enormous mountains. This vacation would be a little different from previous trips.

I usually skied at Park West Mountain, Park City and Deer Valley. Skiing at Park West Mountain was affordable, and it never got crowded. The snow was like in the east with lots of ice and hard packed snow. Hollywood personalities were attracted to Deer Valley, another mountain I enjoyed skiing, because it had a reputation for being an easy mountain to ski at. Park City was my favorite because the variety and length of the runs were fantastic.

In those days, I had a pair of Dynamic GS skis, a ski designed for long turns and ice. On one run, I shared a chairlift with a coach with the United States Ski team. We talked about our past work experiences and, of course, skiing.

After a few runs together, he asked me if I wanted to spend the afternoon watching team practice. I was all in. The three hours watching the best in the world carve tight turns on a steep trail, at breakneck speeds, was exhilarating. Afterwards, he told me that there would be an eight-inch snowfall overnight. He then stated he would like to ski with me in the morning. I advised him that being an ice skier, powder was not in my bag of tricks. But, really, how can anyone say no to the coach of the USA ski team? He said he could teach me how to ski in powder.

We met the next morning; he paid for my ticket, and off we went as the first skiers on the mountain.

After one run, he agreed I could not ski powder, and we amicably parted ways. After waiting an hour until the trails were groomed, I skied the rest of the day by myself. This was an awesome experience!

Returning home to Chicago was a downer, but I was eager to get on with the new year. I was still thinking about some new career opportunity that would magically appear in my world. Over the last year, Robert Wood would constantly call to discuss Thor Guard and the strike out of the blue I experienced at The Northern Amateur. I did not show any interest in working for a company with no leadership and a highly technical product that would be marketable to a non-scientific market.

That winter, after many requests, I agreed to meet with Bob Wood and an investor named Peter Townsend in Chicago. I remember it was cold and snowing as usual. I drove to Schaumburg to meet Peter and Bob. If you haven't already guessed, we met at Studebakers. The meeting was informal, and we spent more time having fun and a little time discussing business. During the three hours of talking and drinking, I agreed to work on a consulting basis for a short time with Thor Guard. There was no way I could see throwing away my comfortable life for a true start-up business. I did not care how great Thor Guard could be in a variety of markets.

In addition, I had less incentive to make a change as G. Loomis Golf was now doing well. They brought in new marketing people to launch the product. These efforts led to selling OEM shafts to Ping, Tommy Armour, Founders Club, Wood Brothers and custom orders for Titleist. Gary Loomis had also moved manufacturing to a new factory that was clean and modern. Everything at Loomis was exceptional, and I expected I would receive a serious employment offer. It would be a dream job because I fished and played golf.

During my visits to the factory, I got along with everyone in the factory because I loved to fish. I could bridge the divide between the fishing guys and the golf guys. The fishing guys did not like the golf guys. Bobby Loomis had a great deal to do with bridging this gap. Bobby had become a good friend!

That February, the Chicago Tribune contacted me. They wanted to do a feature article focusing on my life, but mostly because of my new Dewar's Do-Er moniker. I agreed. The reporter came to my office, took pictures, and explored my past. I did not know what to expect, but I thought they would never publish the article.

On March 17, 1991, issue of the paper, my story came to light. Titled "Profile in Celebrity", the story of my life made me out to be much better than I was. This was a hit! I received an invitation to speak to the honors graduates at Niles North High School that fall because of the article. Even though I had no public speaking experience, I agreed.

With everything going on in my life, I found the time to prepare for a month so I could present something of value for the students. I did not know that so many students, parents, the school board members and academic committee officials would be in attendance. The enormously important task at hand struck me as I entered the stage to begin my presentation. I was nervous beyond description. Thank God I had prepared about twenty-five cue cards to help me remember my thoughts. Everything was going well as I became more comfortable in my role. About half-way through, I dropped my cheat cards and felt like I was destined to fail. At that moment, the rest of my speech emerged without those crummy cue cards, and I spoke directly to the audience. That evening I learned two things: Have faith in yourself and, when giving a presentation, address the audience as individuals. After this successful evening, I grew to love public speaking. I now speak with my audience, not to them!

I had no concrete or useful job offers that year, but I spent more time with Peter Townsend at Thor Guard. Peter had invested a large sum of money with Bob Humphreys to develop a user-friendly system to predict lightning. A word about Peter's background is due.

During this time, I got to learn more about Peter as a person, not just a businessperson. Peter L. Townsend is a true entrepreneur in every sense of the word. He received a bachelor's degree in economics from the Wharton School in 1964. His experience prior to Thor Guard included owning and operating AM and FM radio stations in California and Oregon. Later, he managed marketing commitments for the Osmond (Donny and Marie) family in the United States. He was a Director at Pacific National Bank in Newport, California. He was also involved in developing a partnership between the Fujian providence in China and the State of Oregon.

Prior to his move to Oregon, he attended many recording sessions in Hollywood, California, with many recording legends. After moving to Oregon, Robert Wood had tried to get Peter to invest in the Sona Scan fish finder, but Peter had no interest. However, he saw the life-saving merits of the Thor Guard system and invested. Peter was living on the McKenzie River in Oregon after leaving Southern California for a change in his life. He loved his new home and had no desire to work in Florida on a full-time basis.

One reason for not moving was that Peter and Robert Wood had started a fish fertilizer company in Eugene, Oregon, near his home. This was the primary reason he returned to Oregon. As far as Peter was concerned, he was living in a natural paradise. Miami, Florida, was a far cry from the lifestyle in which he was now living.

Peter and I did not hit it off very well in the beginning. To me, Peter was gruff and would be very difficult to work with effectively. My lack of commitment to Thor Guard contributed to this perception. I wanted a job with Gary Loomis.

The rest of the year was great for me. I directed the Northern Amateur for the last time. I was playing more golf and came to realize that even though I still had a temper; the fuse was longer, and I managed those outbursts better. I still enjoyed my friends and scotch at Studebakers. There were no perfect women in my life, just one woman who was such a disappointment that I permanently discontinued my search for true love. I thought I would live the rest of my life loveless and alone.

Sue and me at Steve Furuta's birthday party

CHAPTER 15

NEW CHALLENGES AND ADVICE FROM A FRIEND

N ew opportunities have always been an exciting part of my life. To this point, I have enjoyed success with Loomis Golf and Thor Guard. I knew that at some point I would need to decide on a future career choice. While the rewards for working with successful companies were personally and intellectually rewarding, I would need to make money again to survive. Even though I had many successes and failures in my past, at nearly forty years old, it was time to find a job that paid well and made me happy. I hoped Gary would hire me at Loomis Golf, but I was still uncertain about any future with Thor Guard.

I needed to make certain that whatever I did had a high probability of success, along with a secure financial outcome. The challenge I saw was that working for either company would mean I would not be the boss. After eight years of operating as a self-employed entrepreneur, making all the decisions and embracing all the responsibilities, I could not see a path forward with either of these two opportunities. I no longer thought that time was on my side.

Gary Loomis came through and offered me a job managing G. Loomis Golf. This was a dream job and my dream job. The dream of an angler and a golfer working for the world's finest manufacturer of fishing rods and golf shafts was appealing. The challenge was moving from Chicago to Woodland, Washington. Overcast skies with drizzling rain were common, daily weather. I liked the sun and warmth of the Chicago summers. I had set my roots in Chicago.

My consultancy with Thor Guard had been going well for me. I was learning from the new L-100 prediction system about the earth's electrostatic atmosphere and how storm dynamics generated lightning-producing energy. I enjoyed the analytical aspect of the system and the demands to understand the system's science and technology. The only way to sell a product is to understand everything about it.

The issues with the system were not in the consistency of accurate predictions of strikes and storms, but with the newly developed electric horns and their inability to function as designed. I knew nothing about radio frequency (RF) communications or communication language, but I needed to have something better and more reliable to sell to customers. Most of my sales were in the greater Chicago and Detroit areas. There was no one to help me with repairs, so I was constantly on the road fixing horn systems. The pay was next to nothing because I was acting as a consultant and not as an employee of Thor Guard. On a positive note, Peter and I got along better, and I believed we might be friends someday. Gary Loomis and I got along well, and we were already friends.

In late fall of 1991, I received another invitation from my friend, Mike Corey. He asked if I wanted to take part in the Steve Garvey Ski Classic in Deer Valley, Utah. The event was to provide resources for the Special Olympics. After all the good fortune I had experienced during our Costa Rica fishing trip with Mike, how could say no? I could stay with my folks and drive to the mountain every day, making easy logistics. During the first day of open skiing, I spent the day with Steve Kanaly of "Dallas" fame. We got along well and skied the entire day together. That evening, we had an informal happy hour where I met the celebrity host, a comedian named Michael Floorwax. With his long, unruly blond hair and "colorful" language, we hit it off immediately. Fast friends and irreverent laughter. Perfect! I went home that evening and told my folks about the day's fun and my day skiing with Steve. Turns out, my mother considered him a great actor and loved his role in "Dallas". The formal reception was the following evening after the ski racing competition. I asked my folks if they wanted to attend, and of course, they said absolutely. Because I had never taken my parents to any kind of party, I thought this could be quite interesting.

Before the party, we had to ski. My first ski race was against Mary Hart, a beautiful actress and friendly woman. She could also ski well. They set up the races on parallel courses, and the winners advanced while the losers were eliminated from the competition. I defeated Mary in a good race. To my surprise, I found out I would be racing against Michael Floorwax next. He could not ski, and I did not want to embarrass him. To make things fun, I paced myself to stay even with the comedian, snowplowing most of the way down the course. About two-thirds of the way down the course, he lost control and crashed into me. We are now laying on the snow, on our butts, laughing hysterically. He had missed a gate, so he lost. At the bottom of the course, ESPN interviewed us, covered with snow and Michael's frozen, long hair. I could hardly talk. I was laughing hard.

Michael displayed a great sense of humor and maintained a perfectly poised demeanor.

After the day's skiing, I went home to shower and dress in my evening party clothes and bring my folks back to the reception. Immediately upon arrival, I introduced my mom and dad to Steve. Mom and dad were impressed with Steve's kind words about their son, and they realized Steve was a genuinely nice person. Everything was going well, and they seemed comfortable talking to everyone, even Mike Corey. Then, of course, they saw me with Michael Floorwax, as we were hugging and laughing. Yes indeed, their son had found the most bizarre person at the party and made friends with him. I heard about that all the way home!

The following evening there was the grand raffle. There were about five hundred people in attendance, and of course, the auctioneer was Michael Floorwax. Dressed in an awful yellow, green and blue paisley suit, he was a riot! During the raffle, people from the audience kept asking him to auction his suit. He kept saying no because it was the first suit he ever wore on stage. Eventually, he agreed and his able assistant, Sherry Belafonte, took the coat and roamed the floor, right to my table. My friends were trying to get me to bid on his minimum one-thousand demand. Sherry had me stand and placed the coat on me. She said, "This is for you"! Guess what? I bought it! One of the most rational decisions I ever made was not telling my folks!

In early 1992, I informed Peter about Gary's Loomis's offer for a dream job and expressed my inclination to accept it. Peter asked if I would reconsider my choice, and I promised him I would. I had not accepted Gary's offer yet, so I needed to find some way to make an informed decision. I needed advice from a trusted third party. My dad was out of the questions because I knew he would want me to find a different job with a big company. I knew I could trust the advice of one old friend, but he was dying of pancreatic cancer. I had no other option, so I needed to visit Gary Adams.

Gary Adams was a true visionary. I may have told him that his metal wood thing was a far-fetched idea, but he never gave up on his dream and made history. Throughout most of the history of golf, manufacturers crafted drivers and fairway woods with beautiful wood. Club heads made of metal sounded like metal and felt hard when striking a ball. Wood was soft, and a well struck shot sounded heavenly. The challenges must have been immense, but he pursued his vision. Gary's wife, Nancy, was truly loving and supportive. Nancy was easy to be around, though she possessed a powerful nature. I admired her for helping Gary through some difficult professional times. His idea of a metal wood changed the game of golf forever. Today, manufacturers make every driver and fairway wood in the market out of metal. The company Gary started, Taylor Made Golf, is one of the largest golf equipment manufacturers in the world. I believe that even though Gary always knew he would succeed; I doubt he ever imagined the future he created would be enormous and so impactful. Gary and I were friends. He knew me well, and so I wanted his trusted opinion.

Gary was in Southern California at home dealing with a horrible, normally fatal disease. I called Nancy to ask if Gary was well enough to see me. Her initial thought was no, but she asked Gary if he was up to a visit from his old friend. He never asked why I needed to see him. He graciously said yes, and that he was looking forward to catching up. Nancy told me to have thick skin because the Gary I knew was not in a body I remembered. We set a date, and I visited Gary after a meeting with Callaway Golf with Gary Loomis. Incidentally,

Loomis was in the testing process with Taylor Made, so Gary Adams knew how good the shafts were.

It was a typical beautiful day in the La Quinta area of California. I found Gary's home and knocked on the door. Nancy welcomed me and told me Gary had a good day but to keep our meeting short. Gary got tired quickly with his illness. I entered the living room where my old friend was sitting in a lounge chair. The man I saw looked worse than anything I imagined. I wanted to cry, but I knew that would make everything worse. He was warm and welcoming as always and apologized for his appearance. What a class act!

We quickly addressed the reason for my visit. I explained that Gary Loomis wanted me to work for him and I also explained more about Thor Guard. I was honest with him and explained my initial decision was to move to Washington and get into the golf business. However, the reason I was in Gary's living room was to get advice from a man I admired and respected as a mentor. Gary did not even need a lot of time to opine.

Gary informed me that Gary Loomis had already achieved success in fishing and golf, and I had already completed the important tasks required of me. Loomis didn't really need me, even though it would be my dream job. Thor Guard would provide an opportunity to affect and save many lives. To Gary, there was nothing more important in life than a satisfying career, especially if a career involved protecting lives. Given a choice, he said that should always be the path to take. Gary then said that I faced the fabled fork-in-the-road decision. Here was the G, Loomis option, a job that would be rewarding, fun and relatively easy. The other fork, Thor Guard, would be the most rewarding job I could ever have, and he knew I would ultimately find success here.

Gary ended with the comment that the Thor Guard route would be the most demanding job I would ever have. He said that remembering the past successes in my life and forgetting the failures would help steer me through the difficult times.

With this advice, I had a decision to make. In truth, I was always going to rely on Gary's advice. I left the house after hugging Gary and Nancy, then cried in the car all the way back to the airport because I did not think I would ever see Gary alive again.

God had a miraculously alternate plan. Gary recovered from cancer and lived another ten years, eventually dying in 2000. Sadly, what happens so often, Nancy died a few months later. However, during those ten years Gary survived, we would visit during the annual PGA Show, share stories and talk about life. He was happy with the choice I made and pleased that Thor Guard was successful.

I made my way home and told Gary Loomis my decision and told Peter Townsend I was now his problem. I had made a hard decision and intended to have success in my new career, a career I never expected to have.

The rest of the year, I continued to sell Thor Guard systems, repair those same systems, and help Gary Loomis when asked to do so. I have always been loyal to my friends, so I helped Gary for a few more years before his new golf staff no longer had any need for my services. I can remember reflecting on my past and the strange way God had placed individuals in my life, along the way, to help me find success in my life, and in His eyes.

Now, the only thing that was missing in my life was, as you have probably already guessed, that once in a lifetime love that would enrich my otherwise lonely life. I was unaware that He was about to change every aspect of my life again!

Once again, I returned to Salt Lake City that Christmas to stay with mom and dad. I knew ahead of time that the discussion of my alternative career choice would come up, but there was always skiing to distract me from dad's critique at the house. When my dad heard of my decision to join Thor Guard, he was not happy. He flatly told me I was just a dreamer going down another path with a dead end. I expected this reaction and explained to him I somehow knew this would be a successful and important venture and that he should not worry about me. The subject never came up again. The five days I spent skiing were fantastic with my mind at ease. I truly became immersed in the beauty of the mountains like I never experienced before. I also skied well and quickly became acclimated to the thin air. In my mind, the year had been part of some distant dream that seemed to become reality. I was now ready to get home to Chicago and begin my new career in earnest.

CHAPTER 16

AN UNEXPECTED BLESSING-AN EARTHLY ANGEL AND A PRINCESS

After a pleasant visit to Salt Lake City, I was now home in Chicago and ready to fully commit to a new professional path with Thor Guard. While I continued to assist Gary Loomis and his team, my anticipation of success was overshadowed by additional concerns.

With two bosses currently overseeing and directing my efforts, a third one would soon be added to the mix. I worked alone for so long and knew my personal path to success, individuals with power who may not like my way of leading and doing things, could interfere with my success. I believed that all the strange associations and people from my past had re-entered my life for a reason. They were there for this job and career. This was my no-fail career decision, and I needed to follow my instincts to achieve whatever it was I was now destined to embrace.

I knew I could work well and respectfully with others. But what if they were overly critical? I knew my new role would have to be aggressive, but sensitive to the demands of others in control. Well, now it was too late; I questioned how much time I should invest in this job. I was still uncertain. Was this the job I was hoping for and expecting? Eventually, I understood, somehow, that this was my forever job and there was no room for doubt! There would be no failure!

From a business perspective, two significant new partnerships would help propel Thor Guard to an industry leadership position. Our team had secured corporate contracts with the PGA Tour TPC network of golf courses and Marriott Golf. My contact with the Tour was Pete Davison. Pete had the vision of creating a safer environment for his customers, employees, and visitors. This was a commitment to lightning safety. No other organization made this commitment. Pete, like Gary Adams, was a true visionary. Pete demanded excellence from everyone who worked with the Tour, but he respected those who worked professionally. We became good friends over the many years we worked together and at his retirement; I gave him an exceptional G. Loomis fly rod.

I developed the same relationship with Kevin Hammock at Marriott Golf. He shared Pete's vision and wasted no time in installing Thor Guard at many of the Marriott properties. After nearly thirty years, Marriott Golf has been loyal to our systems and technology, beyond the framework of our original agreement. In fact, that agreement has expanded into the hotels and vacation club facilities. Marriott had become one of two foundational customers supporting Thor Guard.

The PGA Tour golf course network is a different story. Once Pete retired, the leadership lost his vision and Thor Guard was part of that loss. After twenty-eight years, only a few courses continued to use Thor Guard. I know things often change with new leadership and politics, but going to a competitor whose technology was not in the same league as

Thor Guard's makes no sense safety-wise. I am still grateful, if not disappointed, that the Tour was once part of our family.

February 1st, 1993, was my fortieth birthday. It would fall on a Monday night, a night that Studebakers would be quiet. My friends arrived and all would have a great evening partying. With my lack of interest in finding a new woman in my life, I could concentrate on the stories my friends told. Joey, Jimmy, Tommy and many of the Six-Pack golf group came, not so much to celebrate my birthday, but to party hard! Reaching forty was something I never thought would be a reality. From the time I was in my early twenties, I was certain I would not live past thirty. I viewed this day as a blessing and a surprise. I love surprises!

THE NIGHT EVERYTHING CHANGED

Yes, I spent nearly every night at Studebakers the following ten days. There were no surprises, just uncomplicated fun and drinking with old and new friends. It was strange, as this was the first time in many years I was at my second home, not looking or hunting for women. In all honesty, it was a pleasant change!

Friday, February 12th, would change my life forever. It was to be another regular night with friends and drinking scotch. Most of us knew a blizzard was in the forecast for Saturday afternoon. We seldom went out when the weather was dangerous, so we knew it would be our last night out for the week.

I arrived around 6 PM and met Tommy for drinks and talked about golf. Because it wasn't crowded that evening, we could experience and enjoy the quiet atmosphere. We were at the bar area removed from the dance floor. A stand-up secondary bar surrounded the dance floor.

Around 9 PM, I glimpsed at two women just across from us talking and paying no attention to anyone but themselves. I was not interested in striking up a conversation with either of them because I was woman-free. As the evening progressed, a young, obnoxious whippersnapper approached one girl and began telling her how much he loved her, and he wanted to marry her. She did not know this idiot and looked very uncomfortable. It was cookie night, and I knew I could ask Duke, the bartender, for a cookie hidden behind the bar. He said he had only one left, and it was now mine. I intruded on the engagement talk and acted like this lady was my date for the night. I offered her the cookie, and he got the message. It angered this woman's girlfriend by not bringing one for her as well. This is where it all started!

I was now looking at this girl, Susan, in an entirely new light. She was beautiful. She was impeccably dressed. Her hair was up, exposing her beautiful cheekbones and eyes. About five-foot four, I towered over her slight frame. I was not searching, but as the evening went on, I felt she differed from any woman I had ever met. She was funny, smart and engaging. She told me she and her sister owned a woman's clothing store called Sassy Originals in Bloomingdale, about one mile west of Medinah Country Club on Lake Street.

That night, she dressed as if she had just walked off the runway of a fashion show. I surmised she was wearing what the store sold. We talked for about three hours, then told me she worked in the morning and had to get home. I asked her what she liked to eat, and I told her I would bring lunch to her store the next day. She left Studebakers, and I went back to my friends. The guys were surprised that I was talking to a new woman, but all agreed that she was drop-dead gorgeous.

I woke up late the next morning, hungover. I remember my promise about lunch, but not much more, from the previous night. The snow had already begun falling, and it was getting cold. A blizzard was coming.

Around 12 PM, I went to my local Friday's restaurant and purchased two lunches, a toasted sandwich, and some quesadillas. I drove to her store, a large, old, giant barn on the north side of the road. I proceeded upstairs and found Susan smoking a cigarette in her small office. To say she was surprised to see me would be an understatement. As I gazed upon her, totally sober, she was even more beautiful and classy than I had remembered. We only ate for about half an hour before she said she had work to do. Before I left, she asked if I wanted to come to her apartment to eat our leftovers for dinner. I agreed I would try but told her it might snow too hard for me to make it. She told me to be there around 8 PM. I said that it would work, because church would be over at 5:30 and I would be free. Of course, between 6 PM and 8 PM, there was time to meet Tommy at Studebakers for an early drink. After a drink and a few hits of pot outside by our cars, I went back to my apartment to change. By now, the snow was falling hard and there was already about six inches of snow on the ground. I was nervous about the drive, but I knew my Eddie Bauer Ford Bronco was up to the task.

The weather was terrible. I wondered if I should drive anywhere. As I drove to the intersection of my complex and Algonquin road, I forgot where I was going because I was still under the influence of drugs. It did not matter; I wanted to see this beautiful woman again. I dated many beautiful women in my life, but this one was different.

I drove fifteen miles to her home and arrived safely, but I was freezing. She welcomed me at the door. She had the fireplace burning, a welcome warmth to be sure. The food was on the table, candles lit, and wine poured. Usually, this would mean sex was in the offering. I am all in. I explained to Susan I was a little stoned, but she did not seem to care. She said she was impressed I had gone to church, at which point I explained that I always went to church. We ate, drank and talked for hours, then the bombshell was delivered, with class. She did not want me to drive home, so she offered me the couch to sleep on for the night. I still remember how cold I was all night, with no option available for a warm place next to her in her bed. I must have been blue when I got up the next morning.

The snow had stopped, and the sun had emerged by 9 AM. Susan asked me if I wanted to go to breakfast and I readily agreed. At breakfast, she told me she was going to visit her best friend and husband, Myra and Bob, in Sleepy Hollow. For some reason, she asked me to go with her. I did not want this date to stop, so I agreed with some apprehension. We entered their one-story home, surrounded by snow-laden trees. This was a beautiful setting. The afternoon went well, and I guess Myra approved of Susan's new friend. I dropped Susan off at her apartment with a parting kiss, the first in two days, and went home.

For some strange reason, I knew this was the person I was praying for. Susan thought the same thing about me. To me, it was like an angel princess had entered my life. I knew at the time she had some terrible relationships with her former husband and several boyfriends along the way. I always wondered how she would choose me, a bar hog and drunk, to be part of her life. I will tell more stories about our special times together later but, by the end of that weekend, I stopped drinking and never looked for any reason to leave our new relationship. God had finally brought a soulmate into my life, someone who would be more important than me. I didn't expect it, but it would forever change my life! How could I be so lucky to find my dream girl at Studebakers?

How could I have found anyone acceptable? This entire love story started with a cookie and an idiot. Looking back, I really love cookies and idiots!

The rest of the year was fantastic. Susan and I would spend every weekend staying aboard Head Hunter 2 at Waukegan Harbor. We would fish, listen to music on the boat, visit our boat neighbors, and occasionally play golf. She was mad only one time in our thirty-one years together, and it was on the boat. I played golf with Pat Corey and T.R. Tuner on a Friday afternoon at Big Foot Country Club in Fontana, Wisconsin. This course was hilly, beautiful, and built on some old Indian burial grounds. I could never play well here but loved the course. On this day, things would be different. I shot a 69, four under par and was over the top.

Susan drove to the boat after work and was waiting for me. Because of the great round, I stayed with the guys to celebrate. I was going to be late, as the drive to the harbor was an hour. While Susan was waiting for me, she slipped on the stairs to the cabin and hurt her shin. By the time I arrived, she was very unhappy with me. She should have been. She got over it and we went to dinner. Fortunately, she understood why I was late and forgave me. Afterwards, she told me she was worried that I had gotten into an accident and was hurt. Yes sir, that got to me, and never again did I forget to call to tell her where I was. True love after three months together. Yes, I said it, true love with no searching for her flaws. Those days were over!

The rest of the year went as expected. More horn issues, endless days traveling to repair radios in the horn systems, and days sent selling. Most of my days started at 7 AM and would end at 8 PM or 9 PM. Susan worked most days from 9 AM to 6 PM, so our work times seemed to fit our schedules. I did some traveling to Detroit, Ponte Vedra, FL.

for the PGA Tour and Bethesda, Maryland, for our Marriott contract. Overall, I was happy with my new job and even happier with my personal life.

Susan and I basically lived together, went to church every weekend, and even with our limited financial resources, found time for nice dinners and movies. We traveled to Florida for meetings at Thor Guard. We celebrated our first Thanksgiving and Christmas together in peace. For our first Christmas, I wanted to buy her a special present with the limited funds I had available. I went to JC Penney looking for a piece of jewelry, not knowing what to purchase. I was looking at some necklaces and a very helpful lady asked me if she could be of assistance. I explained our love story, and she selected a gold pendant with a few diamonds on it. I loved it, and so did Susan. She would wear it nearly every day for the rest of her life. After she died, I had a new chain made so that I could wear it as well. It will never be without me!

We watched many movies together that year. I liked children's movies. We rented a movie, "The Never-Ending Story". The movie was fun with a great theme, and the soundtrack was fantastic. So, for Christmas she bought me the CD soundtrack for the movie. It seemed at the time to be a simple, sentimental gift, like a stocking stuffer. Today, it is the most cherished gift I ever received from her, other than her deep love.

That Christmas, we started a thirty-one-year custom. We purchased a Christmas ornament for one another, symbolizing some unique or special event that happened to the other one of us that year.

Today, in our Christmas box, there are sixty ornaments representing everything from new cars to a kidney. Susan had her kidney removed in 2022, shortly after I had colon surgery. I did not put a tree up in 2023, because I just couldn't bring myself to celebrate this annual ceremony alone.

Susan and me in 1993

Susan fishing on Lake Michigan

CHAPTER 17

ANOTHER UNEXPECTED GIFT FROM GOD

Don't worry, I do not plan on writing a chapter for every year following my new life's start with Susan.

There would be too many pages to write and read.

Not that I don't have enough stories and experiences to fill an entire library, I do. However, the significant events that have made my existence full must be told. Life is a cumulative assortment of experiences, each one being significant in some way. Those events, with the greatest impact on my career, enriched my life with understanding and acceptance of God's incredible power and love.

1994 was a busy year. G. Loomis Golf was now the buzz on the PGA Tour and sales to OEMs were booming. Thor Guard was doing very well and had become the leader in lightning warning. Even though we had only one significant competitor during these early years, stories telling of the accuracy of our product and the uncanny ability to perform the impossible, predicting lightning, were spreading.

For another two years, we would struggle with our horns, frustrating me to no end. Fortunately, Susan was always there to encourage me and keep me sane. I was also becoming even more knowledgeable regarding the operational aspects of Thor Guard. Trust: one day in June would put that trust to the ultimate challenge.

The positive reviews about Thor Guard were circulating within the golf business in Chicago. As a result, I was making more sales calls than ever. One day, I received a call from a superintendent at a new private club in Libertyville, Illinois. Oscar Miles had been at Butler National Golf Club in Oak Brook, Illinois, and maintained perfect playing conditions for many years, especially during the Western Open PGA tournaments. Oscar was one of the early pioneers in using computers and other high-tech products to keep his golf course in perfect condition, regardless of the weather. He had heard about Thor Guard and wanted to see if the hype was real. His new club, the Merit Club, was hosting an LPGA Pro-Am prior to the 1994 Chicago Challenge event, to be hosted at White Eagle Golf Club in Naperville, Illinois. Oscar asked if I would bring a system to his event to manage the lightning warning needs for the Pro-Am. I agreed and met him on a nice June day, with no storms in the forecast until long after the completion of the round.

Oscar was friendly and willing to take a chance, but not overly excited about trying equipment with which he was unfamiliar. He drove me out to a remote bathroom building where no one could find me. This location seemed strange to me, as I would have preferred being at the clubhouse. I installed the system, did a preliminary test, explained to Oscar how the system worked, and he gave me a radio in case something needed his attention. He then told me his AccuWeather forecast showed no weather until after 8 PM. Then, he suggested I leave the property and grab a bite to eat at the local McDonald's. Because I already had a Dunkin donut and a large coffee, I declined his offer and remained with my Thor Guard. The club is about ten miles from Lake Michigan. Around noon, clouds moved into the area and the weather cooled with the easterly winds blowing from the lake. There was no appearance of bad weather, so I was not concerned about lightning or having to make a lightning call that would ruin everyone's day.

It was time to get rid of my coffee and donuts, so I went to the bathroom. Two flushes and the water overflowed from the toilet, across the floor and emerged beneath my Thor Guard. Even though the system was on a shelf two feet above the water, my L-100 was showing an increase in activity. I was not sure if it was my bathroom act or a prediction of an actual dangerous weather condition. I radioed Oscar and told him someone had just flooded his bathroom, and a maintenance person needed to come and fix it. For years, I never told Oscar it was me.

I also advised him that there may be a lightning issue, and he needed to observe the system with me. By the time he arrived, the Thor Guard was in high caution with significant amounts of energy nearby. I was now nervous beyond description. I told him that lightning may come, and he needed to be prepared. He was stunned and stood there in disbelief. The readings became seriously high, and I told him that play should be suspended. He radioed Mr. Getz, the owner, Alice Miller, LPGA President, and Mike Waldron, Director of Competitions. With Oscar watching, Thor Guard had gone into a Red Alert.

No one wanted to believe the system, but Alice decided to suspend play. No one was happy with the decision because there was no sign of bad weather. Everyone went back to the clubhouse except for me. I was left in the middle of the course, alone, scared that I had ruined the event for no reason. Remember trust? This was the ultimate test for me.

About fifteen minutes passed with no rain or any rumble of thunder. I was thinking of the embarrassment I would suffer the rest of the day. Then, lightning struck about 100 yards from my location, near Oscar's home that was on the property. It scared the hell out of me! I was pleased that Thor Guard had predicted this unexpected act of God, and I was happy that I trusted the system and spoke up!

The storm lasted about two hours, at which point the event was canceled. I remember thinking that there was no way I would ever play meteorologist again. Afterwards, Alice asked me if I would come to the Chicago Challenge that weekend and play meteorologist again. With great trepidation, I agreed.

ANOTHER PIECE OF THOR GUARD HISTORY

Alice and Mike Waldron warmly welcomed me at the tournament. My weather office was near the driving range, next to a giant electrical generator. Not a great location for the system, but far better than in the middle of nowhere. The first two days were beautiful with no rain and few clouds. When I arrived Saturday morning, the forecast was for another fine day. That thrilled me!

Around 12 PM, Thor Guard showed some activity, low at first but growing steadily. I eventually called Mike to advise him that play would need to be suspended. He checked his radar, then informed me there was nothing of concern. However, after the lightning event on the previous Monday, he reluctantly suspended play. Twenty minutes later, the course was hit by a significant storm. There was little rain but a lot of lightning. Another win for Thor Guard and another nervous call rewarded. Mike was now beginning to believe that the Thor Guard system worked.

Around 2 PM in the afternoon on the same day, Thor Guard, again, began reacting. I advised Mike. This time, he saw some radar activity and immediately suspended play. Sure enough, we were hit by another storm that lasted only about forty-five minutes. I am still happy and gaining some confidence in this new role I did not want to accept. The skies cleared and the rest of the day looked storm-free. At least that's what we all thought!

Around 3:30 PM, Thor Guard was again showing that lightning was imminent. This time, Mike immediately suspended play without question. The storm hit, and it was huge. While I was watching the L-100, it indicated a condition I had not seen before. Because of my knowledge of the system and its operational "quirks", I decided that what I was seeing was a significant wind event. I quickly advised Mike and recommended that the spectators move indoors and clear the tents on the course, which was a good thing because a tornado passed about a half mile north of the club and damaged most of the tents. There were no tornado watches or warnings issued.

I now felt confident about my choice of careers, and I was no longer apprehensive about my decision.

I also had trust in Thor Guard, and so did the LPGA.

Based on what I observed, I knew we could predict tornadoes if, someday, more powerful processors were available. Many years later, the 32-bit processors became a reality for Thor Guard, and we would have an engineering staff who could use this technology. We would be capable of predicting severe storms and tornadoes with an entirely new product. The following year, after the Chicago tournament, Thor Guard would be operational at all LPGA events.

In 1991, at Hazeltine Golf Club in Chaska, Minnesota, there were six people hit by lightning during the United States Open. Even though play had been suspended ten minutes prior to the strike that killed one of the six people, the authorities did not require an evacuation of the golf course.

This tragedy was partially the impetus for the LPGA using our system in Chicago. By 1995, every PGA Tour event, LPGA Tour event, PGA Championships and Ryder Cup events, all USGA championships and European Tour events used Thor Guard. I can confidently say that it was the LPGA and Thor Guard that led to the use of meteorologists and lightning warning systems at every golf event to this very day. Quite an achievement!

Jane Geddes won this LPGA event in 1994, the last professional event she would win in her illustrious career. Jane and I have been friends ever since and I am proud to call her that. She is a smart and kind human.

Oscar Miles would become a member of the Illinois PGA Hall of Fame, a distinction he deserved. His wife Mardel, Oscar, Sue and I would become lifelong friends. On Sunday afternoons, on the way home from Waukegan Harbor and a weekend of fishing, Sue and I would drop off fresh salmon filets for Oscar and Mardel. He loved the fresh fish, and we enjoyed seeing him smile. To me, this was a relationship made possible by all the past friendships and professional associations I had in my life.

CHAPTER 18

THE USGA AND NEW FRIENDS AND CHALLENGES

As Thor Guard became widely known and accepted, along with the reality of providing lightning warning systems at golf courses, golf's most important governing body came calling. Remember my first contact with Tony Zirpoli with the USGA during The Northern Amateur? Strange how some things just seem to reappear from the past. Tony introduced me to Mike Davis, and we discussed bringing Thor Guard to an event for evaluation. In 1995, the United States Open was being held at Shinnecock Hills Country club on Long Island, and I was already in the area attending a Holy Cross class reunion. Great timing for me. A car ride, a ferry ride and I am on Long Island.

In the early days, the USGA would hire interns from Penn State to manage the weather services. They would use whatever systems were available for the job, like radar, lightning detection and weather forecast models. The student meteorologists could forecast well and deal with the easy calls. When it came to those unexpected weather events where lightning comes from a distance, the lightning detection technology they used was incapable of predicting lightning. These strikes required the proven technology behind Thor Guard. We had already proven ourselves on the LPGA Tour and limited exposure on the PGA Tour. This was a great opportunity to show what Thor Guard could do at a major golf event. This was actual pressure!

I arrived on-site to help the interns install the system and train the team as best as I could. Mike made certain that I had everything I needed. I completed the temporary installation and then went to the hotel the USGA staff were using, which was located right on the ocean. My plans were to fish early the next morning in the Shinnecock Inlet, then go to the first practice round of the event.

There had been a thunderstorm that night, but it was long gone by morning. After catching nothing that morning, I went back to my hotel, showered and went to the golf course. As I arrived, I was told that Mike needed to see me immediately. Not good. The storm had hit the club and lightning hit the clubhouse and blew out all the weather equipment, even the Thor Guard. Mike and I met after a golf cart took me to his location. He explained the issue and asked me to help the young meteorologists get my Thor Guard back online.

When I entered the room, I found the meteorologist and his girlfriend taking the Thor Guard apart to fix it. I told them it would not be possible and ordered another system for the next day's delivery. We replaced Thor Guard the next day, but we did not replace the broken detection system. Fortunately, there were no weather issues for the rest of the week. That afternoon, I met with Mike and reported that we were up and running. During our private meeting, he told me what had happened the morning after the storm.

It was hilarious, but the details of his encounter with the two meteorologists will not be disclosed here. I believe this singular incident led to a lifelong friendship with Mike.

Because of this event in 1995, the USGA has never conducted a championship without a Thor Guard, or a Thor Guard meteorologist on site. Mike became the Executive Director, then CEO of the USGA, before retiring and joining Tom Fazio, designing and building golf courses. This was his dream job. Tony Zirpoli retired from the USGA and now provides commentary on rules decisions for the LIV Golf Tour.

The USGA asked me if we could create a simpler, straight-forward system with only four lights representing All Clear, Caution, Warning and Red Alert. At their request, Thor Guard developed the L-50, our first digital system. The USGA ordered ninety-eight of these units for their men's and women's golf associations throughout the country. This was a great example of how two organizations could work together to achieve a common goal. The USGA had quickly become our largest customer and over the years, many friendships would be born and endure.

I was away from home for almost two weeks. I had not been away from Susan for over two or three days in a row prior to this trip. For the first time in my life, irrespective of the value to the company on this trip, I was heartbroken and couldn't wait to get back to Chicago. This new woman in my life had changed everything!

There were also some changes at Thor Guard headquarters. Bob Humphreys hired an individual from a large corporation to handle marketing. This was my third boss. After less than one year, it became apparent that the climate of greed and climbing over co-workers was in this new guy's DNA. I asked Peter to step in and remedy the situation. Peter was also aware of this individual's violation of Thor Guard culture. He was undermining everything we had built and accomplished. He considered himself the only driving force in the company and we would fail without him. Peter acted quickly and removed this person from our corporate lives. Peter had even more of my respect from that point in time on.

Now I enjoyed two bosses, not three. Well, sort of.

Peter respected my instincts, and the success of the company confirmed this. As far as I was concerned, I was part of a team, but wholly dependent on my own efforts. In a way, it was like I was working for myself again. However, this time, I had some experienced professionals there to help me when I needed it. Over the years, my faith in Peter's judgement and financial intellect became central to my success and the success of the company. I knew I had a home and a reliable family of co-workers. For me, everything was moving in a positive direction. However, I was still not satisfied because the horn design had a long way to go before being perfect. Eventually, we would design a new circuit board to help manage the horn operation, but the RF system was poor. Still, I was now believing that this was the career for which I was searching. I thanked God for the opportunity and prayed I would continue to get better at my job. He answered my prayers in spades!

CHAPTER 19

A LOVING PARTNER AND ANOTHER THOR GUARD EVENT

SWEET DEVOTION AND LOVING VACATIONS

The first vacation we spent together was also our first Christmas. We didn't have enough money to leave the cold north for warmer climates. I chose Galena, Illinois, as our destination. We had a quaint hotel in the hills. By the time we checked in, heavy snow had begun falling. The room was rustic, with a fireplace and a hot tub. We spent two nights in relative luxury, and two days roaming around the well-decorated town. We took a break from the pressure of our work and fully enjoyed the quiet time together. Every moment with Susan was a learning experience for each of us. It was becoming clear that we would be a loving couple for a long time. We exchanged gifts, her necklace and my CD of 'The Never Ending Story". While those gifts don't sound extravagant, they were all we ever needed. The small vacation was so special, we returned the next year.

In comfort, we spent many weekends aboard Head Hunter 2. We took a ten-day trip to the beautiful waters of Green Bay, Wisconsin and Door County. We both knew that we would be on a boat, surrounded by water, with no escape if things got tenuous. With a mid-trip stop in Sheboygan, Wisconsin, we spent a few hours in town walking around and having dinner. The next day was another three to four hours to Sawyer Harbor in Sturgeon Bay, our place to anchor for the night. The trip was peaceful, and the evening was fantastic, even though we had only cold cuts for dinner, and Little Debby donuts for dessert. Six days lie ahead to explore this beautiful and vibrant piece of nature. Off we went to the unknown!

Each night we stayed at rental docks in Fish Creek, Sister Bay, and some other nice lake towns. We ate well and enjoyed watching the people walk past all the boats in the marinas. We made boat friends, telling stories of our adventures and our lives back in Chicago. The boat ran well, and each marina had bathrooms and showers. Overall, we were living comfortably in the best room on the lake! After six days, it was time to run the eight hours back to Waukegan. Leaving this life was hard. We were both determined to lengthen the following year's cruise to at least two weeks. On our next cruise, we promised to bring our golf clubs and lighter fishing gear to catch and eat lake perch. The trip home was uneventful, but long.

While we counted the days until our next trip to Door County, we continued to spend all our time together and really became a team. We were both working long hours and crashing at the end of each day with one another. Life was good, and I was experiencing what genuine love was all about.

Susan and I took some small trips together on my work ventures. One of the most memorable trips was when ABC Sports invited me to manage the Thor Guard unit at the 1994 Indianapolis 500 and the first Brickyard 400 races. Susan was not a big race fan, but she loved the sound of the cars and the caravan from our hotel to the track each morning. ABC treated us well and we could not have had more fun. Susan also accompanied me to the Ryder Cup matches at Oak Hill Country Club in Rochester, New York, in 1995. She found it boring but cherished the time we spent together, and I did as well. Too much time together was never enough for either of us.

Our second boat escape seemed to come quickly, and we made the eight-hour trip in one day, again anchoring in Sawyer Bay for the night. Ten days on the lake together would be our favorite vacation of all time. We spent more time exploring and anchoring in secluded bays full of smallmouth bass and yellow perch. We ate more fried fish sandwiches during that time than we ate all year. One day on Washington Island, we played golf. The club said they would pick us up at the marina and take us to the golf course.

Unfortunately, our boat was anchored in Washington Island Harbor, so we needed to take the inflatable to shore, which was about one-quarter mile from our boat. On the way over, Susan's left golf shoe fell into the lake and got soaked. We retrieved it, met our ride, and proceeded to the golf course. The course was a links-style course and wide open. We had a great time and Susan played particularly well. On the way back to the marina, I told her she should always soak her left shoe in water because it improved her play!

We played another golf course further south on the peninsula. Again, the golf course sent a driver and off we went. On the second hole, a medium length par four, I knocked my second shot into the hole for an eagle. Susan thought that was unbelievable but commented that it would not happen again. The next hole was a par five, and I had about 125 yards to the hole for my third shot. I bet Susan $100.00 that I would make the shot, and she accepted. For the second straight hole, I made an eagle and told Susan I expected the $100.00. She reluctantly paid and never bet me again.

We ventured north to Fayette Historic State Park, in Michigan's Upper Peninsula. This old iron smelting center had a long boat dock, looking at the haunted smelting plant. One evening, Susan and I played the Phantom of the Opera CD. Suddenly, a phantom light appeared on the upper floor of the building. There was no floor there, so everyone believed it was the ghost and asked me to stop the music. This was the highlight of our trip.

From Fayette, we traveled to Escanaba, Michigan Harbor and docked next to a delightful couple who were boating across the United States in a twenty-five-foot sailboat. We learned they were only eating yellow rice and nothing else. The next leg of their trip was by overland trailer to the Mississippi River, then on from there. I began casting a spoon in the harbor and caught a large northern pike. Of course, I filleted it and cooked it for Sue and me and our new friends. They shared their rice with us and took the remaining fillets for the rest of their stay. They were so grateful for our generosity. Sharing what you have with other boaters makes such travels worthwhile!

Our trip home was peaceful again, and a new promise for another trip next year. We repeated the same trip the following year, did the same things, but there were no more eagles or crazy bets. In retrospect, being trapped with another person for fifteen days or more, with no escape or ride home, can be a challenge. Susan and I loved all that time together and those vacations would become our favorites. During the trip, Susan found a merry-go-round horse at a store in Fish Creek she absolutely loved, but it was too big to bring back on the boat. In November, I told her I had to go out of town for an overnight business trip and drove to Fish Creek, bought her the horse, and gave it to her for Christmas. She couldn't believe I got it for her and lied about the trip. It didn't surprise me that all was forgiven!

ANOTHER STRIKING EVENT IN THOR GUARD'S HISTORY

Susan knew I was getting angrier every day with the inconsistent horn activations. My days were still being spent between selling and fixing. I had told her Gary Adams was so right that this job would be the most difficult one in my life. I had threatened to quit many times to her, but she insisted I stay the course. Because she was now my rock, I took her advice and endured the torment.

Phil Schwartz, an ABC meteorologist from Chicago, called me on June 18, 1996, asking if I would do an interview with him at Medinah Country Club, prior to the 1999 United States Open that was to be held at the club. I agreed to be interviewed.

On the night of June 18th, a college student, John Scott Wade, was coaching a girls' soccer team in Park Ridge, Illinois, when a storm approached. He correctly ushered the girls from the field to seek safe shelter. About an hour later, as the storm had moved over Lake Michigan about thirty miles to the east, he brought the girls out to resume practice. Just after 6 PM, a rogue lightning strike struck the field and killed John. A genuine tragedy. That evening, the story was everywhere. In one television interview, the Chief of Police assured the reporter that there was no way anyone could have prevented that disaster. I found the comment shocking.

The following day, before the interview started, Phil asked if I had seen the story, and if so, would I care to comment. I told Phil that I would prefer not to be asked about the incident. Of course, during the taped interview, he asked. He asked because that was his job, so I shouldn't have been surprised. My response, not thinking my answer through properly, was that the Chief's response showed the ignorance of people when it came to lightning. I wanted to take my answer back, but Phil liked it. It remained in the interview that aired that evening. The next day, Park Ridge Park District Director Steve Meyer called me and asked if I would come to his office to meet with some folks from the city. They wanted me to explain my arrogant response to the question that should not have been asked. I agreed and expected to have stones hurdled at me prior to the meeting! That did not happen.

The meeting was with Steve, the Mayor and his attorney, and members from various city civic organizations. I explained what Thor Guard does and how that strike could have been predicted, potentially saving John's life. Everyone, including the Chief of Police, reached a consensus that the city should install Thor Guard systems. The mayor and his lawyer stated firmly that a strike like this was so rare, it would not likely happen again. He did not want to spend the money to purchase the system.

Everyone else in the room thought it was a great idea and that their organizations would raise the money, independent of the city. They placed the order with Thor

Guard in November and started planning for an installation the next year.

No company in the world had provided a city-wide lightning warning system at this time. The size of the city would require three prediction systems, L-50 units, and twenty-seven horns. This would be a challenge, especially with my attitude towards our RF system controlling the horns. We also needed to add strobe lights for the hearing impaired. The new Master Alarm Control, the device connected to the L-50, would manage the times of operation of the horns and strobes, manual activation features, and display specific lightning warning levels. I thought I would be alone on this venture, but I was wrong. Steve Meyer was there to help me every step of the way, encouraging me and providing all the maps I needed to design a system that would cover the entire city. We met weekly throughout the winter and smoked many cigarettes. We had a good plan, worked hard to achieve it successfully, and kept our fingers crossed. If you haven't guessed it, Steve, his wife Jan, Susan, and I became lifelong friends.

The plan was to activate the entire system on June 19, 1997, to dedicate the system to John. Over the winter, Park Ridge did a great job advising the public what the various horns blasts meant and when to seek shelter and when it was safe to return to outdoor activities. The entire Chicago press was to be in attendance, along with the four local television stations. Unfortunately, we took longer than expected to install everything and, as a result, we never had time to conduct a city-wide test despite having everything installed and turned on. I was nervous, but the forecast that evening was for late evening storms, well past the operational times programmed into the horns.

Susan and I arrived at the park where John was killed. We met John's parents (very sad) and others who worked to accomplish this massive undertaking. The dedication went well, and when it ended, Susan and I left to find some restaurant for a celebration ceremony. I was tired and totally stressed out! On the way home, we stopped at Sage's restaurant for a bite to eat. As we were going into the restaurant, at about 6 PM, a streak of lightning came from the west of our location and seemed to land around Park Ridge. There was no rain or dark clouds in sight. I paused for a moment, then proceeded inside to have our dinner. When we left the restaurant, the rain was just starting.

When I got home, my answering machine was overloaded with phone calls. Remember those old answering machines? Apparently, that rogue strike, the one the mayor said would never happen again, struck the Hinkley Field scoreboard and blew it and all the lights out at the park. Prior to the strike, the horns sounded and while everyone thought it was a test, the Park Ridge community knew what the loud horn meant, so they all sought shelter fifteen minutes prior to the strike. Fortunately, on this night, no one was hurt. The time of the strike was within five minutes of the time the strike killed John one-year earlier. This strike came from over twenty miles west of Park Ridge. This event will forever etch itself in my mind. The next day, Susan admonished me for saying I wanted to quit. She insisted that there was no option to quit, no matter how difficult the job was. That life-saving warning was all I needed to prove that this was my destined role in life. My God, Susan was so right. I never considered quitting again. One year later, the History Channel produced a show, "Nature-Tech Lightning", highlighting that evening and reenacting the playground games and evacuation.

Foot Note: The L-50 had four lights. Green (All Clear), White (Caution), Yellow (Warning) and Red (Red Alert). The Master Alarm Control also showed four enhanced readings. LHL (Lightning Hazard in the large area of prediction), DI (Dynamic Index (danger of a strike close by), FCC (Energy discharges in the entire range of the system), and AD (Countdown to a safe resumption of activities).

Sue and me leaning against the brick wall

Fayette harbor building

Door County Sunset

Me and the big pike

Sunset

CHAPTER 20

TRANSITION, COMMITMENT AND LOSS

The events surrounding Park Ridge brought a new mindset that would endure for many years. I now realized that Susan was right, and this was the career for which I was searching. I dreamed of a path forward with a strategic plan for products, concepts and services I had never even contemplated. The learning curve ahead would be steep and difficult, but I now had an attitude that there would be no failure in my future, or in the future of Thor Guard. These next few years there would be a series of tests, tears and change I was not expecting. So is life as we are told!

TRAGEDY

In the summer of 1999, I had gone to visit my folks because my mother was not feeling well. She had issues with sciatica for many years, so the doctors told her. During my stay, she had a series of specialized blood tests performed and learned, from those tests, she had leukemia. A tornado caused the destruction of the exhibit booths at an outdoor recreational convention in downtown Salt Lake City on the day she received her diagnosis.

My dad tried to find some cancer center to help but could find none that would take her. I called an old friend with connections. He sent a jet and MD Anderson in Houston admitted her the next day. The day she left for the airport, I also left for a national sales meeting with a partner, DTN (Data Transmission Network), in Omaha, Nebraska. Our companies combined forces and Thor Guard supplied a small prediction system, the L-25, for their satellite radar computers. This business had significant importance and Thor Guard was used at all NCAA championships for several years.

That evening, I arrived in Omaha, Nebraska, and my father called me in great pain, informing me that my mother had died shortly after they admitted her to the hospital. The news hit me hard. The next morning, I relayed the news to the company president, Reed Moormeier, and told him I would leave later that afternoon, missing most of the meeting. During the morning session, a detection competitor was speaking to the sales personnel and trashed Thor Guard and our technology.

The previously dormant volcanic temper was threatening to erupt. Reed could see this and ushered me out, only after admonishing this individual for his comments against a major supplier to DTN.

I flew home to Susan and planned mom's service, then tried to figure out what to do with dad. We would plan for a mass and a burial service in Albany a month later.

My dad asked me to provide the eulogy and play the piano during the service. He requested "Wishing You Were Here Again" from Phantom of the Opera. I hit only one unpleasant note, the last note of the song. That was for mom! The eulogy went well, uplifting with some of my strange humor. I have done several eulogies, none of them were tear-jerkers on purpose.

The next few days, Susan and I took dad for rides in the area, including a long trip to Fort Ticonderoga in upstate New York. Even with a stop for my dad's favorite ice cream, he was hopelessly devastated.

Unfortunately, all too soon, I would be exactly where dad was in a dark black hole!

Susan and I spent Christmas at home in Illinois. Despite our enjoyment of some snow and cold weather, this year the forecast was for no white Christmas. We knew that New Year's Eve and New Year's Day were going to be in the upper forties and the ground was free of snow. We decided it would be fun to play golf on New Year's Eve, 1999, then again on New Year's Day, 2000. It was too cold to play eighteen holes, so we went to Thunderbird and played golf on the front nine on the last day of 1999, then returned the next day, the first day of 2000, to play the back nine. We were happy to say goodbye to 1999 and looked forward to fresh adventures in the 2000s! In retrospect, our first seven years together seemed to be too good to be true.

A MOVE AND A CHANGE IN OUR LIVES

In 2000, Peter asked me to move to Florida to assume the management of Thor Guard in Sunrise, Florida. He told me that if I didn't move, he would have to find someone other than me to run Thor Guard. Clearly, that was not an option, so I agreed. Fortunately, the city of Bloomingdale had attempted to take some land from Susan's store for a new road. That would leave Sassy's with no customer parking. The city bought the building and the business, leaving Susan and Anne with a nice profit. Now Susan was free to move with me. I did not want to move to Florida's east coast. Susan was getting excited about moving away from Chicago. Oddly, if you haven't guessed it, we flew to Florida and began looking for a house on Marco Island. Even though it would be an hour and a half drive to the office for me, we wanted to live in paradise.

Our house hunting trip would only be for a few days. Eventually, we found a model home we liked and a lot that was affordable. We went back to the builder, gave him our plans, and he informed us the house we liked would not fit the lot we chose. With no time left, I visited a friend of mine from the island, Dave Stonier, and asked if he knew a realtor who could help us. He was renting space to one, introduced us, and off we went. We told him our budget, and, with sadness, he said that there was only one house in that range, but he had never been in the house and knew nothing about it. What option did we have?

We arrived at the house, one of four houses in the cul-de-sac. It was beautiful. Susan went into the house, and I went to the backyard to see how much water we had on the canal. I was stunned to see about 200 feet of seawall! I didn't care about the interior of the house because I was sold. I entered the house and told Susan this was the house we were buying. She expressed some concerns regarding the wood floors, but we had no choice at this point. We made an offer, then went to church that evening. While we were at church, "Amazing Grace" started playing and at that moment, we knew we had found a new home. Remember, my mom's name was Grace, and this was the church my parents attended when vacationing on Marco Island. By fall, we moved in, although

Susan really moved in because I was attending the Six-Pack Open in Chicago. She was not happy with me, but she did a great job coordinating the relocation without me.

ANOTHER BLESSED DECISION

Prior to my mom's death, I needed to find a representative to replace me in Chicago. I knew this would be difficult because I built this territory and treated it and my customers as my own. I would be very picky. My old friend, Walt Wynarczyk, contacted me to ask for a job, purely by coincidence. He had left the golf business and was in an awful place. I did not think that hiring a friend, especially one with no experience in my business, was a good idea. After great thought and deliberation, I offered him the job. As if this was as God intended, Walt would become the most successful representative in Thor Guard's history. I later learned from his wife Diane after Walt's death from pancreatic cancer that he was on the verge of suicide. In retrospect, God saved us both!

A wonderful couple bought my boat in Illinois, Head Hunter 2, the year after we moved to Marco Island. With the proceeds, I purchased a nice bay boat for fishing and sightseeing trips in the Gulf of Mexico and the backwaters of the Everglades. This boat would never become our new home away from home. There was not a bed or a shower, so it was a day boat.

The move was now behind us, so I thought it was time to propose to Susan. I know, I know, what took so long? Just me being me. I purchased as big a diamond as I could afford. One afternoon, I asked Susan if she wanted to go for a boat ride to Coconut Island, a small coastal barrier island at the mouth of the Marco River. We found a secluded beach, beached our boat, and went for a walk on the soft, white sand. While she was looking at the Gulf waters, I got down on one knee and waited for her to turn back in my direction. Looking down, she saw the ring and nearly fell over. I asked, and she said yes. As Catholics, both of us being divorced and not wanting to go through the annulment process, we put the marriage off for sixteen years. We were eventually married by a fantastic priest on Memorial Day, 2018. I was sad because it took too long, for all the wrong reasons. Even with this delay, we were more in love that day than the day we met. Every day with Susan was pure ecstasy.

The following year, I saved up some money to purchase a new diamond for Susan's ring. The diamond she had was beautiful, but I wanted a larger and more perfect stone. A few weeks before Christmas, I asked her if I could take her ring to the jewelers to have the setting checked and to have it professionally cleaned. She agreed and off I went. Her diamond had already increased in value, so I selected a larger stone of higher quality. The stone was beautiful, like my Susan. I picked it up a few days later and returned it to her. She commented that the cleaning really worked, and the stone looked much larger than before. Later, I told her it was a new stone and a sign of my love. She was thrilled and asked if I could get her ring cleaned every year. She never wanted a larger diamond, thank God! It was a great Christmas on paradise island. Susan was never big on receiving expensive gifts, but for this time only, she was all in!

Susan had done a beautiful job decorating the house, placing pictures everywhere, and selecting beautiful area rugs around the house. Because of her eye for fashion and interior decorating, our house was now a comfortable home. Throughout the following years, she would continue to do her magic and improve every aspect of the house. Susan and her daughter even redesigned the kitchen with little help, even going so far as cutting southwest tiles for the counters. They both worked hard, and the results spoke for themselves.

Everything came out perfectly!

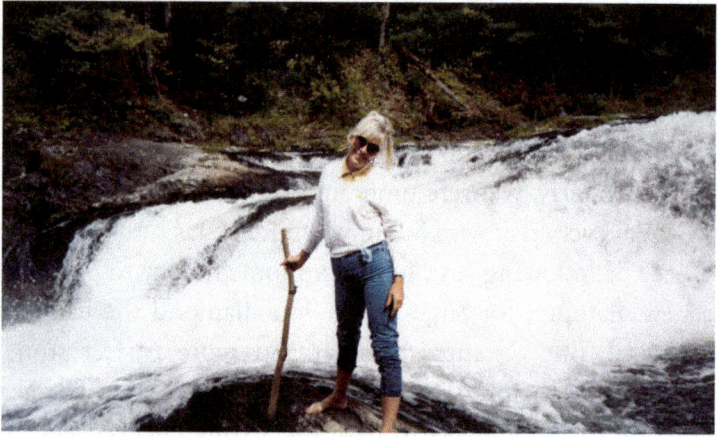

Sue at a waterfall in New York

Sue at Lake George, New York

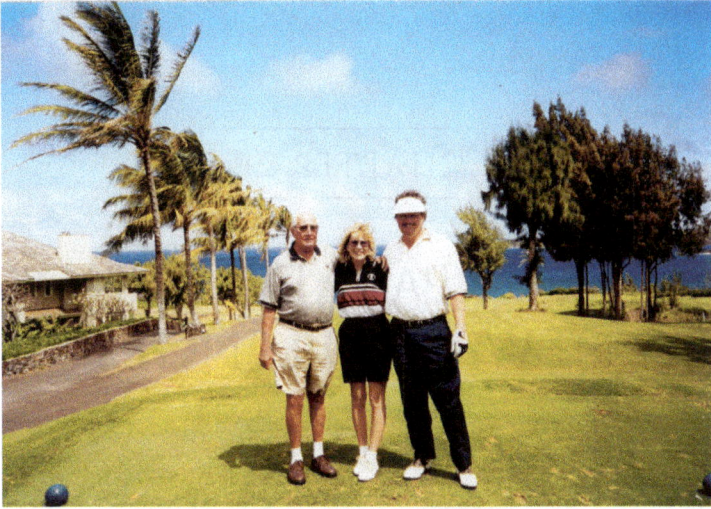

Sue, me and dad at Kapalua

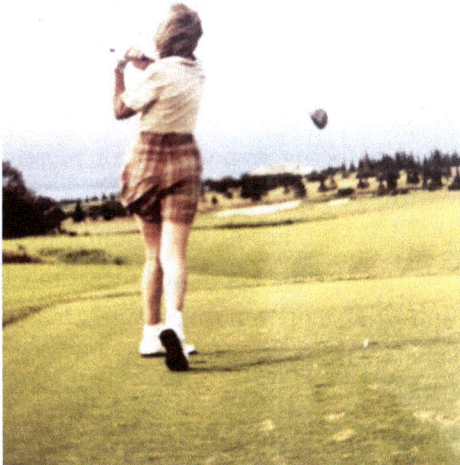

Sue driving at Kapalua

CHAPTER 21

LIFE IN PARADISE AND NEW CHALLENGES

BUSINESS

S hortly after moving to Marco Island, FL., Peter promoted me to President of Thor Guard. That may sound like an exciting event in my life, but I was now responsible for the success of the company and over forty employees and sales representatives. Thor Guard founder and inventor died unexpectedly a few years earlier. Now Peter and I oversaw the company, and my responsibilities included, well, everything.

I was used to being responsible for myself. I was not comfortable with the prospect of managing others along with overseeing the development of complicated technologies. It would take me years before I accepted the simple fact that the employees and sales representatives were a team, and Peter and I were their coaches. I could not do everything, even when everything needed to be done. Once I grasped that concept, I would become a calmer and better person.

At home, I always knew I had Susan. She was my source of strength and humanity. I doubt I would have been successful without her daily encouragement. Whoever said there was an exceptional woman behind every good man, they were right!

After working with Peter for over ten years, our relationship developed nicely, both personally and professionally. Whenever I needed him, he was there to help and offer advice. This would come in handy for me and the company in the future.

John Kluge, Peter's stepfather, who was once one of the richest men in America, took a controlling interest in Thor Guard after offering financial assistance in the late nineties. John had a controlling interest in Metromedia and had made most of his money in radio and television. He liked Peter and me, and he was always encouraging our efforts to make Thor Guard a very special company. His board members were not as encouraging. After John died in 2010, the board members, along with their 51% ownership of Thor Guard stock, became overbearing and critical of our efforts. They did not like me and pushed Peter to fire me multiple times. Fortunately for Thor Guard and me, Peter would have nothing to do with their demands. It is a good thing that Peter kept me in the dark for many years as to their hatred of me, because things would have been very different. My temper would have come out of the closet! After years of reporting to the board, Peter and I would buy our stock back and fire them! Since that removal of greed and hatred from our environment, Thor Guard has grown and prospered beyond our realistic expectations. Once again, God stepped in and saved the day for everyone.

At Thor Guard, each day brought its own set of challenges, but it also provided many opportunities for personal and professional development. I had a strategic plan that would take our products and services far beyond lightning prediction. For many years, we worked with a company who performed forecast services for the USGA, PGA Tours and the LPGA. After losing those contracts, except for the LPGA, we hired two of their meteorologists and assumed the contract for the USGA, a contract we have kept ever since. We bid on the PGA Tour contract and won. However, they did not inform me of some expensive strings attached until after they awarded the contract. As a result, I withdrew the bid.

Knowing the next in line for this contract was our previous partner, whose new leader did not believe in Thor Guard's technology, I advised the Tour that the Thor Guard systems they relied on for so many years could no longer be used. I was concerned that the system may generate a lightning warning, and they would not consider it valid. If a tragedy occurred because of this lack of trust, someone could drag Thor Guard into a costly lawsuit. In hindsight, the decision was right, and the USGA became our most favored forecast partner. One of the two meteorologists we hired, Jake Swick, has become a valued member of our leadership team and manages all our forecast services.

During these ten years, we developed two new systems, the L-150 and the L-75. The L-75 would remain the foundation of our product arsenal for another seventeen years. In 2007, I worked with a company called Pegasus to develop an entirely new RF system for our horns. Finally, after all these years, we had a system that would stand up to the ravages of nature and deliver both a horn alert and strobe message to the remote horns without error. I admit, I enjoyed being engaged with engineering projects, especially when they were successful! I was now feeling comfortable with the title of president and excited about the new product and technology ideas I had for the future. This was the career I had always dreamed of and never expected.

Besides my work with Thor Guard, in 2004, Gary Loomis purchased his special rolling machines for golf shafts back from Aldila. I got Gary and Bobby Loomis back into the golf shaft business, along with several investors. We began building shafts again, but only to be used in metal-headed woods. The shafts were great but prone to breakage. Failing to fix the problems, we folded a few years later. This was my fault. If we made shafts for irons, the company would have been a massive success.

Because the irons shafts were thicker in the tip, breakage would never have been an issue. It taught me a valuable lesson: stay in your lane and rely on experiences and intuition to guide you.

PRESONAL LIFE

Life on Marco had been amazing. Throughout the year, Susan and I made new friends and had a great time fishing and playing golf. She spent a great deal of time visiting her mother, Mary, in Orlando, then later visiting her at the senior home in Naples. Susan would donate her time at the home teaching the seniors, arts and crafts and other fun and some challenging projects. Her stories of the elderly guys trying to do things their own way and messing things up were hilarious. She really loved her time there and giving back with pleasure. I was happy to see her so happy! She also spent time in the library finding new movie videos and bringing them home for our entertainment. She said it was difficult for her to select movies we hadn't seen, but she enjoyed taking the time to find a few winners. Susan also enjoyed reading books from the library as well. Susan's good friend Debbie, at the library, would share movie and book recommendations all the time. I can't remember a single day or evening where she was not reading a new book. Whenever we were on a long trip in the car or on the new big boat, she was reading.

Many people on the island are part-time residents, making the search for friends difficult. We found Sue and Chuck Thomas, and Chris Crossan.

Chuck Thomas lived across the canal from us. My next-door neighbor knew Chuck and introduced me to him. Chuck was a lawyer and coincidentally, I was looking for new legal counsel for the company. On my way out to fish one morning, Chuck was cleaning his boat, and I introduced myself and told him about my legal needs. He was a senior partner with a national firm and introduced me to Cheryl Wilke, manager of the Ft. Lauderdale office. Cheryl was a bulldog, an aggressive advocate on our side. She was great. Chuck and later his wife Sue, would become lifelong friends with Sue and with me. We would visit them at their family home in Lake Geneva, Wisconsin, and when they were on Marco for the winters, we would play cards and have frequent dinners together. Chuck was a hot air balloonist, pilot, boater, jet ski fanatic, and a troubled golfer. Sue was a calm and lovely lady who volunteered at San Marco church.

Chris Crossan was the battalion commander of the Marco Island fire department. One evening, my neighbor's air handler sounded like it was about to blow up. I called 911, and they dispatched the fire department to follow up on my concerns. One firefighter walked onto the neighbor's dock and looked at the tarpon resting under the lights. I came out on the porch and told him those fish were off-limits because they were mine to catch. When he got back to the fire station, he called me to follow up on my 911 call and we talked for hours. That evening, Chris became one of my best friends, someone who would come to my rescue years later.

By now, I had experienced boating in a big way around the island. After using the small bay boat to explore the Ten Thousand Islands, it was time to get another big boat for longer trips to places in the Keys, Sanibel Island, and the Naples boat harbor. I was lucky and found a thirty-five-foot Cabo, equipped with a tower, at a donation group in Ft. Lauderdale. The boat was perfect and half the market price.

Fortunately, the boat's design was perfect for rough waters because every trip we took, either going to or coming back, had very rough seas.

On our maiden voyage from Ft. Lauderdale to Marathon, one of the northern Florida Keys, we faced constant four-to-six-foot waves. Susan handled it well and did not complain. I felt frustrated! The trip from Marathon to Marco was no better. The boat, named "Thor Cast", took us to some great destinations, creating fresh memories along the way. Unfortunately, these trips were not the same as our uneventful Lake Michigan and Door County trips. We owned "Thor Cast" for nearly seventeen years. In the end, I spent more time working on the boat and far less time using it, so we sold it. I was sad to see her go, but now I had more golf time for Susan. She loved her golf, and I loved seeing her have fun playing!

We enjoyed a new tradition for New Year's Eve and day. We would take the boat to the Naples Yacht marina and spend two or three days staying on the boat, using the showers in the club and watching whatever movies Sue found at the library for our evening entertainment. There was a seafood restaurant connected to the complex, so the location was perfect for a New Year's dinner and celebration. There were two notable evenings I will never forget. The first New Year's

Eve, we got a table for a seven o'clock reservation and sat next to a lady and three men from North Carolina. The lady was quite entertaining, especially when she crushed a cockroach on her table and followed up with the exclamation "damn critters"! That would have made the evening, but it wasn't over. The special for the evening was lobster Thermidor. The server brought their food, and although it looked fantastic, the lobster was not cooked. They returned their meals and waited for their replacements. We had also ordered the lobster and when they served it to us, mine was cooked and Sue's was not. I gave her my dinner and waited for a cooked version of the delicacy. No one got mad, but the evening was full of fun as we became part of our neighbor's outrageous laughter. After our entertaining meal, we went back to the boat, climbed up to the top of the tower with wine in two plastic glasses, and watched the evening fireworks. This was an exceptional and loving evening.

The following year, we made reservations at the same restaurant, now under new ownership. There were about twenty tables in the restaurant and this year's dinner would be different. Sue and I had the table for the entire evening. We had an appetizer and went back to the boat to smoke. We returned and had our salad and left again for a walk. Again, we returned to sit for the main course and had a casual meal with no roaches in sight. We went back to the tower on our boat with our wine and watched the fireworks. We returned for dessert. It was now about ten-thirty and time for another break. We took a walk along the river, then returned later for champagne. It eventually took about four hours to eat.

Sweet memories indeed!

We would bring our bikes on the boat so that we could bike to the pier, to breakfast and lunch around town. We would bike for miles. While we were there, most of the time, there were no issues. Occasionally, Sue would have a difficult time turning and lightly crash into a nearby bush. She never got hurt, but I always had to look behind me to make sure she was upright. She seemed to find all the bushes!

Sue and I would spend a few more New Year's celebrations at the harbor until we could no longer find a slip to rent. Regardless, we had truly found paradise in Florida and with one another.

Sue with her big snook

CHAPTER 22

WORLD'S LEFT BEHIND

When you think you have found peace, it is amazing what unfolds in life's journey. Many aspects of your life soar and the sins and hardships of the past become buried in distant memories. In my case, I have become more confident in every aspect of my life and the fear of failure is no longer part of my present. I credit this sense of well-being to my love for Susan, my strong relationship with Peter, and the ongoing support of my growing sphere of friends surrounding me. I have adopted my father's management style, keeping respect and humanity as part of my daily life. I have become confident in my understanding of Thor Guard and the products associated with these life-saving systems. I have also come to understand genuine compassion watching Susan interact with her mom, Mary. The love and friendship they shared made me sad I did not have that depth of a relationship with my mother.

Unfortunately, there is no remedy available to go back in time to fix things. If a time comes along in your life where you want to go back and correct the past, death makes that journey an impossibility. Learning this so late in my life is tragic, but not repeating the sins and omissions of my past has become the path forward.

Sue and I have settled into certain routines we follow every year. We typically spent Thanksgivings in Salt Lake City with my mom and dad. After my mother died, we went there less often, opting to spend this holiday with Susan's mother and sisters. This was great for Sue but left me somewhat hollow inside. I loved Sue's mom, however, and enjoyed her company. She was a hoot!

During the time between Thanksgiving and Christmas, Sue and I would watch the same movies each year. Starting with Planes, Trains and Automobiles, we would move on to watch Christmas Vacation, Camelot with Richard Harris, Love Actually, A Christmas Story, Phantom of the Opera and The Sound of Music. Every December 22nd, Susan and I would sit by the tree and exchange our gifts with a glass of wine. We would move to the lanai and have a cigarette with our wine, then settle in to listen to Christmas CDs. These included the Christmas albums of Celine Dion, The Carpenters Christmas album, John Denver's Rocky Mountain Christmas and finish the evening marathon with Kenny Login's Christmas album "December", our favorite. The next day we would drive to Merritt Island, Florida, to spend Christmas with her daughter Kim, granddaughters Hailey, Samantha, and Kaitlyn. Then later with her great grandson Gavin. Most Christmases were without chaos. Sue and I would return to Naples on December 27th to prepare for the New Year. I looked forward to this break from work with the anticipation beginning on my drive home from work on the 22nd. Christmas was our favorite time of the year and yes, we kept Jesus in the celebration. Susan's mom would always be with us.

Our world changed in March 2012, when Susan's mother, Mary, died. Her family came to Naples to be with her at the hospital while they waited for her death. Late that afternoon, Mary sent all her children away for dinner, but had Susan stay behind. An hour later, Mary passed away while only Susan was present. That is how Mary wanted to die, with her closest living daughter with her. I knew this was a tragic loss for Susan, yet I never saw her shed one tear. For a month after her loss, I would hug and comfort her every day and ask how she was feeling. She would tell me she was very sad and missed her mom deeply. Even with all this pain, there were never any tears, at least in my presence. To this very day, I never understood this side of Susan!

Sue and I went to Salt Lake City to visit my dad and his second wife, Barbara, for the 2013 Thanksgiving Day celebration. My dad was not doing well and earlier that year, his sister Ruth died. Her death was sad for me because I truly loved her and her husband, Uncle Jim, who died in 2003. It was equally difficult for my dad, especially because he was not well enough to travel to Albany, New York, for the service. We celebrated Thanksgiving and, mostly, enjoyed the five days spent with Dad, Barbara, and Barbara's family. I was not comfortable with my dad's condition, but Susan kept me positive every moment of our trip. When things got quiet, Susan and I would drive to Park City for a coffee and pastry. We loved going to the mountains to be alone and in awe of the snowy beauty of the area. During this time with dad, for the first time in my life, he told me he was proud of me, especially the work I had done with Thor Guard. Every son is always hoping for a father's expression of love and admiration for his son's noble life and successes. I was no different!

Susan and I had been home for less than a week when Barbara called me on the evening of December 6th to tell me that dad had died. So many losses in a year! When my mother died, I was not feeling the intense sadness I thought I should have. When dad died, I felt the same way. Strangely,

I believe that my adoption played a role in this because when my mother died; those intense feelings of sadness I thought I should have had were missing. I am not sure I will ever understand this part of me! I now wonder if this was a normal or abnormal reaction to these events.

BUSINESS EVOLUTION

We had not improved our lightning sensor since 1985. Our customers would refer to them as salad bowls. In effect, they were! They needed cleaning four to six times a year. I designed a new sensor that worked well and required little maintenance. At least, that was the plan. We had one representative who had constant issues with the system not operating as designed. His systems did not work right. He later sued us in federal court, claiming we misrepresented our product to the government. Oddly, other customers were not experiencing significant issues, but we spent a great deal of time looking for answers. Regardless of where we looked, there were no obvious answers to these issues. We spent years looking for an answer, then this representative recruited one of our prized meteorologists and employees to join him in the lawsuit. Personally, this was hurtful because I had nurtured both individuals. Because I designed the sensor and fully understood the technology behind it, my intuition led me to believe the issue was not in our technology but was somewhere else. With all of this going on, Thor Guard was still growing, and our position in the market was notable.

I became restless with our current technology and wanted an updated system packed with all the goodies I dreamed we could create. This new system would transform our company and our industry. Thor Guard hired a new engineer, David

Redanz, and he would help me take my dream to reality. A fast learner, David, understood what our Thor Guard could do and understood how we analyzed the electricity in the earth's atmosphere. I was excited that I had an engineer I could trust and believe in. He covered all the bases, so to speak! Before the end of 2015, we had a successful circuit board design so we could begin testing. I began designing the new system enclosure. After naming the system TG 360, we relied on Jake Swick and his staff to begin work on the software. The plan was now in place and underway. I was determined to succeed and with God's help, we would!

Susan with her mom, daughters and granddaughters

CHAPTER 23

MORE LOSS, SOME AGGRAVATION AND PURE JOY

As I have aged, I realize that my perception of time has changed. Time passes so fast now that it is hard to comprehend that even a minute, an hour, or a day feels completely different from when I was 10. Time just seems to speed by-even though it really doesn't change. Sometimes this is a blessing and at other times, a curse. It seems like only yesterday that I lost my dad and Sue lost her mom. It now occurs to me that while things around me are changing with astounding speed, my mind just does not keep pace. Time is everyone's curse!

The next five years in my story will test my limits of sanity yet reward me for perseverance. To me, logic no longer applies in my life, only a belief in God and a comfort that comes with faith.

The new Thor Guard TG 360 is now undergoing live-storm testing and performing better than I had ever hoped. The engineering team has followed through with my vision and created the best product Thor Guard has ever produced.

It truly is better than any weather prediction technology on earth. The relief I felt from success would provide me with some level of comfort and satisfaction I had never experienced before. This confidence would carry me through some difficult times to follow. A rapid succession of personal and professional blows would come sooner than I would have liked. Such is life, I guess!

By mid-2016, my uncle Ray, dad's brother, would die after a prolonged heart condition. Billy, his only other brother, was killed on the beaches of Normandy during World War II. With this loss, there were no other Dugans alive. If Sue was not in my life and a source of great strength, I would feel like I was in a large room surrounded by sadness. Even though I was adopted, the loss of my "adopted" family left me feeling empty. I was just getting over this loss when another one hit me.

In December 2016, my best friend and Thor Guard's most successful representative, Walt Wynarczyk, died of pancreatic cancer. This was the same nasty cancer that took my friend Gary Adams. I knew Walt was ill, we all did, but he kept the seriousness of his illness from his friends and wife. One day, I called to see how Walt was. I knew they had admitted him to the hospital for something. I called his cell phone, and his lovely wife Diane picked up the phone. I asked how Walt was, and she told me he had just died. She asked why I called at that very moment, but I had no answer. To this very day, I still do not understand why I called her moments after his passing. I wish I had called a day or even an hour earlier and could speak to my old friend and wish him well.

Time presents another problem in that it cannot be rewound. Every minute that passes is gone forever! I wanted to go to his funeral service, but a blizzard in Chicago, Illinois, had all planes grounded. I could not make it to my friend's last farewell, as mother nature defeated my efforts.

The following year, 2017, would prove to be another year of Thor Guard's success and personal heartache. A well-lived life can make a person wise, but as age wins out, our bodies fall apart. This is man's lifelong struggle and without faith, it is an insurmountable challenge.

I released the employee and the representative who were giving the company problems. I saw pictures of a few of this representative's Thor Guard installations. He was violating all of Thor Guard's installation directives required to ensure that every system was safe and operating perfectly. Every one of our representatives must follow these procedures. They are not options. I realized the reason he was having so many issues and jeopardizing the lives of the people depending on the system for safety was that his installation practices were doomed to failure. Even though we were still looking into the sensor issues, his failures had nothing to do with the sensors. After his termination, a plan initially endorsed by Peter and the members of our New York Board, we all knew the probability of getting sued was high. Over the next few months, I received additional pictures of his work, which confirmed my observations that his work was the issue. The sensor was never the issue!

After I took this action, I continued to respond to his threatening emails. I considered responding professionally was the smart thing to do, but New York said to stop altogether. I did not respect these board members and followed my intuition to calm things down; I knew the chance of success was very low as this person had a temper, something I could relate to. I hoped logic would make him retreat, but he only got worse. Things would come to a head soon with him, but sooner with New York!

One fall afternoon after I came home from work, Sue carefully told me that her tests revealed a small mark on her right breast. I could tell she was worried, but did not want me to be overly concerned. The following week, we would go to an oncologist to receive the final verdict of her condition. Neither Sue nor I ever had any physical ailments, so this was new and raw for both of us. The following week, we would be told she had a small tumor in the breast that would need to be removed. Before the doctor walked into the examination room, Sue had a seizure and needed to be brought back to consciousness. I was freaked out, and the doctor was too. I bribed her with a Dairy Queen Blizzard on the way home, always her favorite, and that helped a little. Now it was time to look for a surgeon to perform the procedure. After seeing the first doctor, who had not even taken the time to look at Sue's mammogram, simply said the entire breast would need to be removed. We told him what we thought, and after he finally looked at the pictures, agreed. After this encounter, he would not be our surgeon!

Soon afterwards, I called my doctor, Dr. David Linz, and he recommended a female doctor he had heard good things about. We made an appointment with Dr. Sharla Patterson. Unfortunately, hurricane Irma nailed Southwest Florida, delaying the procedure until October. Our initial visit with Sharla was perfect. Sue liked her and so did I. She informed us that Sue would need a lumpectomy, followed by radiation. This was a more humane surgical procedure and done by a caring person.

The following two weeks I spent cleaning the mess Irma had left us. The pool cage was destroyed, and the pool was full of large branches and leaves. Sue wanted me to have our pool service clean the pool, but I insisted on doing all the work. Eventually, everything was back to normal at our home.

One day in October, we left early for the hospital for Sue's outpatient procedure. On the way, I received a call from New York that I reluctantly took. With both of us being preoccupied with the procedure, taking this call was not the best decision. I still answered. I explained I was driving Sue to the hospital for breast surgery to remove a cancerous growth. They did not care! The conversation became heated, and I respectfully said goodbye and hung up. Sue was grateful I left the conversation, one-sided as it was, and we continued to the outpatient center. The surgery took about three hours, while I waited in the waiting room for the results of her surgery. During that time, along with being concerned and nervous about Sue, I determined our New York problems had to go. These heartless souls had no place in my life.

Sharla came out and took me to a private consultation room. She informed me that the procedure went well, assuring me they had successfully removed all the cancerous cells. Upon hearing this great news, I gave her a big hug and called her our angel. She seemed appreciative, if not somewhat surprised, by my act of gratitude.

Sue finished her radiation treatments and was cancer free. I suggested Sue may want reconstructive surgery because her breast was slightly deformed. She did not want another surgery. I was fine with her decision and impressed she did not care about her looks, nor did I. My love for my princess was boundless and not tied to looks. I believe, however, that it bothered her because she wasn't perfect. I never addressed my feelings on this matter. If she was okay with the way she was, I was as well. I would have supported any decision she made.

The following year, our New York directors would literally force us to buy them out. Their demands started in late February. We bought them out in May, and the two disgruntled representatives filed a lawsuit against us in June 2018. I believe Metromedia knew we were being sued, but they kept Peter and me in the dark. Peter and I assumed this was the case afterwards, but we got our stock back at a higher price than we would have offered if we knew what they apparently knew. Nevertheless, Thor Guard was no longer under the thumbs of these tyrants! We were free to run the business, our developments, and pursue our future the way we wanted.

Soon after our purchase, the two representatives were terminated. Their case never went to trial and the following year, the case was settled. Not a single government customer of Thor Guard came forward to support their baseless claims that Thor Guard systems were unsafe. They were perfectly safe when operated and installed properly. Another ugly Thor Guard chapter gone in the wind.

Shortly after the purchase, R.A. Miller, our founder's partner and accountant/ manager of Thor Guard, left the company she had worked for from its inception in 1973. Peter and I accepted her request that we purchase her sizable number of shares. Peter and I now had a controlling interest in the company we built and were ready to take our baby forward without interference from anyone.

If you recall, shortly after moving to Marco Island in 2000, I proposed to Sue. Being Catholic, neither one of us wanted to go through the long annulment process. We were both divorced, but wanted to be married by a priest, not some government official. Our friends Chuck and Sue Thomas introduced us to two of their friends, Rick and Amy, who knew how we could be married by a Catholic priest. After an hour-long meeting with our new friend, Father Tony, he agreed to marry us. We had a private, intimate ceremony on Memorial Day, 2018. We chose that day because we had so much fun at the Indianapolis 500 and I could never forget our anniversary. Afterwards we had a nice dinner at the Watermark Grill with Tony, Rick and Amy, then made our way to the Sanibel, Florida Marriott for a brief, two-day honeymoon.

Upon our arrival, the hotel staff gave us a warm welcome and guided us to a two-bedroom suite with awesome views of the Gulf of Mexico. Waiting for us were champagne and chocolate-covered strawberries. Marriott management made our two evenings with them magnificent.

The following day we would have breakfast in the gulf-front restaurant, then drive to the Sanibel Country Club for a round of golf. The day was beautiful, and we both played well. Afterwards, we drove to the next island called Captiva and had ice cream cones. I was hoping the day would be perfect, and it was. Later, we went to the Lighthouse for dinner and shared a bowl of lobster bisque. Dinner was shrimp for Sue and swordfish for me. By the time we returned to our room, we were full of food and exhausted. We finished the champagne while having a smoke on the balcony, watching the day's sun sink into the sea. I promised Sue we would someday have a real honeymoon somewhere special. Regrettably, I never fulfilled this promise.

On our brief trip back home, we stopped at Mel's Diner in Estero for breakfast. Afterwards, we stopped at a used high-end car dealership and looked at Ferraris, McLarens, and Cobras. I loved sports cars, having owned a Porsche Carrera GT in the seventies. The cars were all beautiful, thinking that someday I would own a supercar once again.

In retrospect, I wish I could relive these days with my new bride forever! After twenty-five years with Sue, I never looked for flaws in her character, as I had done with others in the past, and we never argued or fought about anything. I regretted waiting so long for our perfect relationship to be officially sealed with God's blessing. I also regretted that her mother was not alive to see her loving daughter married to her soulmate. Regrets are the mark of omission!

Dad, Aunt Ruth and Uncle Ray

Our wedding day

CHAPTER 24

LOSS AND ENLIGHTENMENT

2020 went by with few earthshaking moments. We were very lucky. The business was doing well, ending the year with record revenues. They were not significant; however, they proved the new TG 360 would be a success.

We got through the worst of the Covid pandemic, with no deaths to our immediate family and friends.

Sue had fully recovered from her surgery. At the end of the year, Sue insisted we each get the Covid "jab". This went against my instincts, but she was worried that if we caught the China virus, we would die. I did not want her to get the shot alone, so I joined her. Early the following year, we got the second shot. I had a serious reaction and was sick for a week. The stories of heart problems had not yet reached the press, or at least the free press, so we were unaware of these potential side-effects that were so dangerous. We moved forward, assuming we were now fully protected from the virus. I remained uncomfortable about our decision.

Peter took more time to be with his wife Penny, taking trips and spending time at their beautiful home on Lake George, New York. He kept his position as Chairman of the Board and passed the CEO moniker to me. This time, I felt like I was fully prepared to handle the additional responsibilities. I employed a great engineering team and a talented CFO, Jason Wolk, who took R.A. Miller's position. I learned much from Peter over the years as partners and understood how to run this business, and did so with the lessons my dad had instilled in me. Sue and I never celebrated the advancement, but there was no need to do so. We were just happy for this opportunity and that twenty-eight years of effort finally paid off.

I had no plans to retire soon. However, now that I was making good money, I began saving as much money as I could so that when my retirement came, we would have plenty of money for travel and the freedom to go where and when we wished. After working so hard all those previous years, I owed a beautiful and worry-free retirement to Sue, my angel princess. Every wish I had held in my heart was finally coming true. My temper was gone, my harsh words with God were all in the past, as were my failures. I now had gratitude that I grew into a successful human being. Life's winding road was now making sense to me!

In June, I finally sold "Thor Cast", and watched it leave my dock for the last time. It was a bittersweet moment. She was a great boat and when we could go on cruises, Sue and I were grateful we had her between us and the water. The sunny side of seeing her go was that I would no longer be spending my weekends cleaning her and providing the constant maintenance necessary to keep her running. Even with all the cuts on my arms and hands, working in close quarters below deck, I will never regret owning a truly fantastic vessel.

Things were going well for us until October, when Sue Thomas notified us that her husband, Chuck, had died of a heart attack after attending a wedding in Maryland. The news hit Sue and I hard.

There had been so many loved ones dying that another close loss was devastating. My Sue would bring Sue Thomas clam chowder and chili throughout the winter while she was in town. We would take her to dinner, trying to provide solace. She was a strong woman, but Sue and I could see the pain in her life every time we went out or visited. Sue and Chuck had seven children and sixteen grandchildren. That support network was there for her. It was invaluable!

One granddaughter shed some light on death and what comes next. Graciela is autistic with a talent few people will ever enjoy or embrace. She does not speak but communicates with the use of a special computer to relay her thoughts. Graciela writes well and is extraordinarily intelligent. Her gift is being able to communicate with the souls who have left this life on earth. For example, the family was at church one evening and Graciela was sitting next to an elderly woman. She took the hand of this woman because, somehow; she knew the woman was very sad. As it turned out, the woman had recently lost her husband, and she smiled at Graciela. The granddaughter never enjoys being touched or touching others. No one ever saw the lady again. Graciela refers to her as Ester Williams. We will never know who she was or what her name was, but who would question Graciela?

Graciela had other communications with the dead. She described how her grandfather was having a difficult time passing over the void between earth and Heaven. She explained how she helped her grandfather, along with many angels, make the successful transition. These words were inspiring for Sue and me. Her writing reinforced our belief that Heaven is real and our friends, relatives and many others exist there in grandeur, love and extraordinary peace. I never believed in this sort of ethereal communication, so I was skeptical, but her words seemed to make everything so real and believable. Fortunately, I did not know what was coming my way!

In October, my doctor was concerned about my elevated PSA. I had some tests performed with results expected by December. I also replaced my ailing Lexus RC 350 with something new and exciting. With the help of my friend Chris Crossan, I found a Chevy dealer who would help me order a new Corvette C8, hoping to receive it in less than a year. Used C8 Corvettes were selling for more than double the sticker price. Purchasing a slightly used Corvette was out of the question. I ordered the red metallic mist color and settled in for a long wait. Sue loved the car and was hoping my dream would come true before the expected delivery date promised by the dealer. It seems like everything worthwhile never comes fast enough.

Thanksgiving came and our plans were for a home alone day. We watched our movie on schedule as always. However, Sue Thomas invited us to spend Thanksgiving dinner with her family and we readily agreed. She asked us to come and bring nothing in the food category. Not us! I fried a turkey, and Sue cooked her most excellent sweet potato casserole, a better tasting dish than Ruth Chris's. She also cooked her cheesecake to boot. Sue enjoyed cooking and she was an excellent one. The house was full of family and some neighbors, and the one thing in excess was food. Everyone ate well, and it was a fantastic evening, even without Chuck.

The week before Christmas, Chris Crossan and I went out fishing for a few hours. We caught trout. A lot of trout. As we sat on the lanai after cleaning the boat, I received two phone calls. The first was my doctor telling me I did not have prostate cancer. Within minutes, my car dealer called to tell me the Corvette would be delivered by the end of the month. What a fantastic way to end a great day of fishing and a year full of challenges.

Sue and I shared another great Christmas with her daughter Kim and her grandchildren and great grandson. On December 31st, Sue and I went to the dealer to take delivery of the Vette. Man, it was beautiful, almost too nice to drive home. After completing the paperwork, they gave us a tutorial on the car's computer and then we loaded up for the ride home. Sue commented that even the small Toyotas around us seemed high because we were so low. I admit I was nervous driving home, hoping to avoid any type of collision. We made it, then showed off a bit by taking the Vette to a nice New Year's dinner at a local restaurant on the island.

At year's end, Thor Guard had been blessed with another record year. The new system was selling well, and another new model was on the drawing board. Sue and I were both looking forward to a fantastic 2022, healthy and happy.

CHAPTER 25

REIMBURSEMENT DELAYED

2022 was the year that I promised myself to spend some quality vacation time with Sue to make up for being away so often. Even though we spent all our time together when I was not traveling or commuting to the office, we seldom had the time to just escape for a week alone, together. After nineteen years, I owed it to her in a big way.

Sue never complained about anything. She assumed that our reward for the years of hard work would result in some away-from-work discovery time together. At least that was the plan, not only for this year, but for many years after. On a personal note, I was looking forward to spending this time with Sue more than anything. Now that Thor Guard was on firm footing and profitable, there was no reason to delay my plans any longer. Well, at least that is what I thought!

My doctor had encouraged me over the years to take a variety of tests to catch any potential health issues early. I eventually succumbed to his demands and had all the tests done except one. I don't know if most men feel this way, but the idea of a team of doctors sending a device up my butt was just one test I did not want. At sixty-nine years old, it was time for my first colonoscopy. I didn't see the value of this embarrassing procedure since I had no symptoms whatsoever. I still scheduled the "invasive" procedure for April 15th, months after my birthday. Some present this would be!

If you have not had a colonoscopy, you spend the day and evening before the procedure drinking a gallon of nasty stuff to clean your colon. This was an awful experience but clearly (ha!) did the job. Once at the hospital, the nurses take you in for prep and you strip down before they stick needles into your veins. There you wait to be wheeled into the cold procedure room. They instruct you to roll over on your side while administering the injection of happy drugs. Within seconds, you are gone. Then, as if time just disappeared, you wake up in recovery and wait for the doctor to tell you everything looks great. At least, that was what I was hoping.

The doctor came into my room and showed me a picture of an ugly, massive tumor blocking ninety percent of my descending colon. I initially thought that this was someone else's picture. I was then told it was cancerous! Neither Sue nor I was prepared for this bad news, especially because Sue had blood in her urine for several months, and those doctors could not determine the cause. Her health was always more important than mine. I thought I could wait on my "fix", but the doctor insisted I needed immediate surgery, or I would surely die.

An appointment was scheduled with a surgeon the following week. The doctors had already ordered a biopsy of the cancerous tumor. I visited Dr. Ryan Obi, and he confirmed the tumor was cancerous and needed to be removed, along with six inches of colon, or I would die. He took the time to describe the procedure and tried to allay our fears of a bad outcome. If there was to be a human digging into my body, this was the man I would choose.

I checked into the hospital on Friday, May 13th, for the main event. Sue would wait in the waiting room for the three-hour arthroscopic surgery. I was concerned she was more worried than she let on, and while waiting to be wheeled into the operating room, with needles in both arms, I could think of nothing other than what she was going through.

I knew I would come out of this trial unscathed, physically. It is always the emotional injuries that heal the slowest. Unfortunately, the tumor was extremely difficult to remove, and the surgery lasted for over five hours. Sue was justifiably worried because she was left uninformed about anything that was transpiring in the operating room. The doctors successfully performed the procedure, and they wheeled me into a nice recovery room overlooking the Gulf of Mexico. I woke up on Saturday afternoon and they provided me with what they claimed was lunch. This was the worst, tasteless food I had ever experienced. Sunday evening, I was released from the hospital and Sue drove me home. I was sky high and did not even remember the ride.

The week before my surgery, Sue had a CT scan performed on her kidneys to determine the cause of her bleeding. She had her follow-up appointment with her doctor scheduled for May 17th. Fortunately, her daughter Kim was driving from Merritt Island to attend the appointment with Sue because I would be bedridden all week. I did not want Sue to go without me, but there was no way I could accompany her. I knew Kim would be perfect for the role.

As if things weren't bad enough, Sue found out that the CT scan showed a spot on the lower portion of her right kidney, requiring the kidney's removal. We were both stunned! In a follow-up meeting with her surgeon, an appointment I could attend, the surgeon confirmed our worst fears. Loving my sweetheart as I did, I wanted to seek a second opinion prior to her scheduled July 19th surgical appointment. On June 22nd, we traveled to Tampa's Moffitt Cancer center for a second opinion. During this visit, we learned Sue had a second kidney on top of her primary kidney, which was rare. The consensus was that the kidney needed to be removed. Our ride home was hard and quiet. I was devastated by the news, especially because her surgeon was heartless and a robot. The only positive aspect was that he possessed a wealth of experience with this intricate surgical procedure.

So, the challenges continue. They discovered that the cancerous blob in my colon was encapsulated and there was no other cancer detected. You know the drill, good news and bad news!

During one of my follow-up visits with Dr. Obi, I included Sue and asked him to explain her procedure and the actual functions of kidneys. Her surgeon did not do this for us. Dr. Obi took the time to carefully and lovingly describe everything and assured us that Sue's surgeon was very good at his job. That helped immensely! Not only is he a brilliant doctor, but a skilled surgeon. As far as I was concerned, I healed quickly and was back to physical normalcy within one month. Lesson to be learned here. Get your colonoscopy early to avoid the trauma I endured.

Sue had her surgery. It went well, and she healed physically. I say physically because she was not happy and seemed to feel depressed. This was not the Susan I knew. I took time with her and tried to help emotionally, but to no avail. Seeing her like this was depressing for me, particularly because nothing I did helped. I felt truly helpless!

I had a series of business trips planned for September that would have required me to be away from Sue for two to three weeks. I couldn't do this to her or to me, so I asked if she was up for a road trip. She knew where I had to go, so she agreed. Chicago, here we come!

We rented an SUV and drove to Chicago. I had to attend a show and a USGA event at Erin Hills, Wisconsin, as well as a LIV Tour Event at Rich Harvest Farms just outside Chicago. Sue could spend the time with her sister, the one with whom she owned Sassy's. The trip was long, but I believed getting away from Florida and spending time with her sister would help. I believed it helped. Sue and I were eager to get home. Our return trip took us to Irmo, South Carolina, for two days of business meetings. We had some sumptuous dinners, then left for her daughter Kim's house on Merritt Island, Florida. We spent two days there and Kim helped her mom relax. By the time we got home, I was hoping everything would get back to normal. Not so fast, buddy!

We were finally home on September 25th, and Hurricane Ina hit three days later. Unbelievable! The wind was not an issue with this storm, but the ten-foot storm surge was. Water came one foot from entering the house, as the surge completely covered seventy percent of the island. It took weeks to dig up our shrubs, plants and small trees that the salt water had killed. Again, Sue did not want to see me working so hard, but to save $1,000, I was determined. When I finished, I told Sue I should have paid someone else to do the work. Sometimes I can be unreasonably stubborn.

Sue flew to Burbank, California, to celebrate her daughter and granddaughter's birthdays, as she had done for twenty years. This was additional healing time for my princess. Everything went well, and she returned happy and relaxed.

We spent this Thanksgiving with her sister in Cape Coral, Florida, and Christmas at Kim's. The restaurant where we ate after our wedding, Watermark Grill, was the venue for our New Year's Evening dinner celebration. We took the Vette, dined early, and got home before the drinkers hit the road. We spent the evening with champagne, listening to music and watching a movie. In retrospect, it was a perfect evening, especially after the crap we went through all year long.

The good news is that Thor Guard significantly shattered all previous sales revenue records. It is difficult to appreciate our blessing during a year like this, but we were healthy and together. I couldn't ask for more than that!

PART THREE

CHAPTER 26

HIGH HOPES

Sue and I were looking forward to an exceptional year with our health issues behind us. Being the sensitive and loving woman she always was, Sue was looking forward to our lives together in our seventies, eighties and nineties. I would tell her I may not be so lovable in my nineties! Sue would say she didn't care because we both would probably be mostly brain dead by then. She would always put a positive spin on everything. She was perfect in every way I could imagine.

We, or I, decided the house needed painting. To prepare for the house painting, we had a roof cleaner visit in mid-January to do his thing. Although we had not selected a color for the house, this job was first on the list. Once done, the rest of the process would be interesting. There was a nearby house with the color and trim Susan really liked. Eventually we selected a color that was acceptable, and shortly after the roof was done, we had the painter visit and then signed a contract to paint the house. The earliest they could start was April, but the job didn't begin until mid-May. Susan was excited to update the outside of the house, but really wanted us to remodel the master bathroom. She may have felt disappointed that we didn't prioritize the bathroom remodel. But she never complained.

We had an annual routine after moving to Florida. We would drive to Orlando a few days before the start of the PGA show to drop off items needed for the show. On the way to Orlando, we would stop and play golf at one of many golf courses, selected depending on which route we took to Orlando. Later, we would continue to Merritt Island, where Susan would spend the week with her daughter Kim. However, this year would be different. Kim and her sisters Anne and Theresa would go on a cruise while I was working at the show. Kim and Sue would gamble, and the sisters would attend shows. Little did they know they would never see Sue again! I remember driving them all to the boat and continuing to the show to set up our booth. I would then drive to Sarasota to have dinner with Kevin Carpenter and others from Attitude of Gratitude. This was a long day and by the time I got to our show hotel, I was exhausted.

The show went well, and I returned to Kim's house and later picked the girls up from the ship. As expected, Kim and Susan made some decent money playing blackjack. Everyone had a great time, ate well and got home safely. Then Sue and I went back to Marco Island for a slight break. The following weekend, we would play golf and follow that routine every weekend into May. Sue seemed to do better and was a happier person. I intended to spend more time at home and cut my travel schedule in half. I owed it to my princess.

Sue and I always celebrated the anniversary of our meeting in Studebakers on February 12th. We would each select a nice place for dinner and spend the evening just being together. We did this for thirty years, with no exceptions. This was belatedly followed by a February 1st birthday dinner for me, then another birthday dinner for Susan on her birthday,

April 25th. It may not sound like these celebrations were a big deal, but they were. We always felt so blessed and lucky to have found one another and believed it must have been by the hand of God we met. After all, the odds were against our meeting ever happening, no less falling in love.

My next trip was to Orlando for the LIV Tour event at Orange County National. I went for a few days and returned for my last CT scan after my surgery. At the end of the month was my follow-up colonoscopy from a year earlier. This time I was clean and agreed to a follow-up procedure in three years. They also found no issues in my CT scans and decided not to schedule any more. Things were looking up!

We had a pool leak that was severe. On May 1st, the leak detector came and determined we had a leak under the concrete deck requiring some major surgery. We scheduled Red Rhino to repair the leak on May 19th. My schedule included traveling to Tulsa to meet with Tulsa schools to attend a LIV Tour event on the week of May 9th. Sue really wanted to play golf, so we played at Royal Palm in Naples on Friday, May 5th. Susan dropped me off at Ft. Myers International Airport on the morning of May 9th and proceeded to Costco for some shopping. I called Susan when I arrived at Midway in Chicago, as I waited for my last leg to Tulsa. She sent me a text with two hearts and said she got home without incident. Later, I called from Tulsa to let her know I was safe. She is always worried about me.

We always talked several times a day when I was traveling. On my drive after the school meeting, I got lost on my way to the hotel. I called Susan several times, joking about getting lost because of my car's on-board navigation system. I finally found my Holiday Inn Express and crashed for the night. I returned home on May 13th. Sue picked me up at the airport and we had dinner by the airport before returning home. Susan was in great spirits and happy to have me home. I was happy to be home as well.

Even though we were together for over thirty years, this coming Memorial Day would be the fifth wedding anniversary. In the past, we would go to our favorite restaurant on the Isle of Capri. We knew the owners well, and the food was exquisite. After they closed, we substituted one favorite for another in Naples called Truluck's. They would take great care of us and end our dinner with a baked Alaska, on- the-house. We made a reservation for Sunday, May 28th, at 5 PM. We were looking forward to our special time together, celebrating a special day that should have occurred many years earlier.

On Friday, May 19th, Red Rhino came to start their work to fix the pool leak, and the painters arrived to start the house as well. It was a busy day at the house, but by 6PM, everyone was gone. The following day, Sue and I would play golf in the morning before going to church for St. Finbarr's four thirty Mass. Normally, Susan would always finish eighteen holes, but this round she quit after sixteen holes because it was so hot, and she was tired. As always, we held hands going into church and leaving after mass. In fact, like teenagers in love, we held hands everywhere we went! After church, we went to Burger King for our normal after church lite meal of a Jr. Whopper cheeseburger and water. We returned home and had a normal, quiet evening watching television.

The following week was normal - at least the first four days. Susan had received a call from her doctor saying her heart artery scans were good and there were no issues to worry about. Sue was always quietly worried about her health. The painters were busy at work. I went to our Sunrise, Florida, office on Monday and Thursday. Susan and

I would go out to dinner on Tuesday night, another night out for a break. I had golf planned for Friday morning and Saturday with my friend, Chris Crossan. When I got home from work on Thursday, Sue was waiting at the door as I pulled into the garage and a big hug would soon follow. This was a normal welcome home every time I came home from work, running errands or playing golf. Susan had tried a new recipe containing ground beef and rice. Appropriately, they were called porcupine meatballs. These gems looked like a ball with spikes emerging from the ball of meat. It was quite good! Around 11 PM, we went to bed for the evening, but Susan had a hard time falling asleep. Normally, I was the one who had a hard time sleeping!

INCONSOLEABLE ANGUISH

At about 3 AM the next morning, Sue collapsed on the kitchen floor and later woke up, not knowing what had happened. I woke up around 7 AM and she told me what had happened. I asked why she didn't wake me, and she said that she did not want to disturb my sleep. I was upset with her and suggested we go to the emergency room immediately. She already had a doctor's appointment scheduled for late morning and she insisted on going there instead. She liked her doctor! I should never have listened to her this one time. When Susan had a plan, she stuck to it and this time, things were no different.

Early that morning, Susan and I sat on the lanai to have our morning coffee and a cigarette. While we were talking, a beautiful cardinal landed on the screen enclosure and stayed far longer than normal.

Occasionally, a cardinal would rest on the enclosure for a short time. Susan's mother, Mary, loved cardinals and

153

whenever Susan saw one, she took it as a message from her mom that she was doing well and looking after her. This time, the cardinal stayed far too long. Later, I took this as a message from Mary that Sue would soon join her in Heaven.

We left the house around 10:30 AM. The painters had finished the front of the house, but there were still plastic sheets around the windows. I asked Susan how she liked it so far, but she did not seem interested in commenting. I should have immediately realized something was terribly wrong. Before arriving at the doctor's office, we stopped at a Shell gas station just around the corner to pick up a carton of cigarettes. Sue always bought her cigarettes at this store. We lit up and drove around the corner to the office. We finished smoking and walked into the office, holding hands like always. She seemed to be doing better now and had some life in her stride. We arrived a little early, waited about fifteen minutes, and went into an exam room to wait for the doctor. He would come to visit about five minutes later. As with every doctor's appointment, she was nervous.

The doctor spoke with us for a while before taking Sue's blood pressure, then checking her heart.

Susan's blood pressure was ninety over sixty, but the doctor said her heart sounded normal. He suggested that an intravenous flow of fluids would help her feel better and raise her blood pressure. That would be the last plan.

We went to another room with a nice reclining sofa where Susan would lie and receive some fluids intravenously. She looked tired. As usual, the attendant had a hard time finding a vein that he could pierce. He finally found one in her hand and began the drip. I stayed with her for half an hour until she told me to go to the nearby Aldi grocery store to get some cranberry juice. She really liked the brand they sold. She told me we would get coffee later and go home to rest after her appointment. I was supposed to play golf that day and I canceled my tee time to be with her. She said that after we got home, I should go out and play nine holes, and she would ride with me. I told her I loved her and would be back soon. Never did I realize I would never see her alive again.

I drove to Aldi's grocery store and bought juice and some cream-filled cupcakes to eat with our coffee. As I got into the car, I got a call that read "scam". I took the call. It was the doctor's office telling me to get back to the office immediately because they had called 911 for Sue. I couldn't imagine why they needed 911, but they didn't provide me with any more information.

When I arrived at the office, the emergency vehicles were already there. I went into the office towards the room Sue had been in and the doctor stopped me. I could see the paramedics providing CPR and working hard to, as I later discovered, bring her back to me. I asked the doctor how bad it was, and he said, "it isn't good". Shortly after I arrived, they took her to the hospital up the street, the same hospital in which her mother died. I followed behind, but the sirens weren't blowing, and they were in no hurry. That is when I began to understand that she was dead. To be accurate in the description of my situation, I was in shock! I couldn't cry or remember any part of the drive. I parked and went into the emergency waiting area. I would sit there for at least an hour with no information concerning the condition of my angel princess. Eventually, a nurse took me to a consultation room and told me the doctor would be with me soon. The doctor came in and I do not remember if he introduced himself. He told me that my wife had died, then asked me how she died. I thought this was a strange question, but I informed him she died in her doctor's office while receiving an IV. He was cold and seemed uncaring. He then left and said someone would be back to take me to Sue. About fifteen minutes, the nurse's aide came and escorted me to the room Sue was in.

I entered the large, cold room. Before me was a shape beneath a white sheet, lying on a cold, stainless steel table. I drew back the sheet to see my beautiful wife lying motionless before me. She looked so peaceful and beautiful. I was now beginning to cry excessively. Her eyes were slightly open, so I opened them so I could see them better. Her irises were radiant, shimmering with gold and silver accents. I had never seen eyes so beautiful! I spoke into her ear several times, "come back to me", a line in "Somewhere in Time" that just came to me without thinking. Of course, she did not listen. For forty five minutes, maybe longer, I hugged her and tried to bring her back. Her white sheet and my blue shirt were soaked with my tears. I felt helpless! Never in my life had I experienced being plunged into such a black hole. I wanted to change places with her and tried to wake up, as if I was in the middle of an awful dream. Nothing worked. I noticed a bag with her jewelry in it. There was her wedding ring, her pendant I had given her at Christmas over thirty years ago, and a watch I had given her at Christmas years earlier. I took the bag, and some clothing left behind and after taking a last look, I left the room. Outside the room, I looked for someone to speak with to say that I was leaving. No one paid any attention to me.

Eventually, I grabbed someone to advise them I was leaving. They simply said OK, with no condolences provided. It was like the way they saw my dead wife was just another dead body. Heartless. I will never go to this hospital for any reason in the future.

The memory of Sue lying on the table and all the details from those moments will stay with me forever. I have tried but I can't un-see them! Even worse, I never got to say I love you or kiss her before she died. She died alone. I will never get over this!

I went to the car and reluctantly called Kim to tell her that her mother was dead. That call did not go well for either of us. Something special occurred with this call to Kim. Something special still lives in our relationship eight months after Sue's death. This was a blessing that took months to comprehend. I can only assume I feel this way because Sue is a part of Kim, and I seem to feel that whenever I am with her.

I drove home carefully, because I knew I was in no shape to drive. I was in shock! When I got home, seeing the newly painted house, I broke down again. I found myself lost. Instead of going into the house, I went to my neighbor's house and told Ellyn and Francisco that Sue was dead. Ellyn hugged me as I cried, but my pain was there to stay. I eventually went home; a home Sue had been responsible for beautifully decorating. That evening, I saw Sue had left her side of the bed turned down, and after a long prayer session, I slept where she had slept for twenty-three years. I did not sleep at all, but I had nowhere to go and no one to talk to. I was more alone than at any time in my life!

The next morning, I went to visit the harbor at the Esplanade. There was a cold east wind blowing as I drank my coffee, smoked and talked to Sue. She would not answer my one question. Why did she have to leave me? It was 7:30 AM and after being there for an hour, it was time to go home. Home to what? This place was now just a house.

I was planning on leaving from the north exit so I could turn north on Collier Boulevard to go home. There was another exit to the south with a stoplight, but I chose the easy way out. The traffic at that hour of the morning was so heavy, I had to turn right, proceed to the stoplight and then make a left the back way past Winn-Dixie and Veteran's Park. Very inconvenient. As I was passing the empty park, a white Mercedes was backing out of a spot, so I let them out. Through my soaked eyes, I noticed the license plate, it read "HEAVEN". After twenty-three years on the island, I had never seen this plate and I have not seen it since. I took this as a message from Sue saying that she was safe and happy. I never imagined that for many months to come, there would be more signs and miracles intended for my soul's resurrection.

Later that afternoon, Kim and her daughter Samantha drove four and one-half hours to the house to console me. I will never forget the painful hug I shared with Kim as we cried hard tears. Samantha was sad as well but was unsure how to behave. After thirty years of knowing Kim and watching her grow up, I had never seen this side of her. She was empathic, caring, and inconsolable. It made sense because she and her mother were best friends and confidants. I was sorely in need of something extraordinary to help me through my desolation. I had never felt more alone. Kim did her best to help me and she continues to work hard to keep me centered every day.

The rest of the week would have me at the harbor every morning. On two of those visits, there were single and double rainbows. Rainbows are truly beautiful if you see them in the correct light! One morning at home, I forgot to place the coffee cup under the coffee maker. Of course, there was coffee everywhere but in the cup. I had to laugh because weeks earlier, Sue had done the same thing and wondered how she could have made such a mistake. I cleaned everything and told her no one was perfect except me. So here I was, Mr. Perfect, with coffee everywhere. It seemed appropriate, perhaps a message from Sue.

Two days after Sue died, I found a book she had partially read. She had only finished two chapters. I am sure her friend Debbie at the library suggested this book for her to read. For the next week, I read "It's One of Us", by J.T. Ellison aloud to Sue so that she could finish her book. When I finished, I took the book back to the library and asked if I could buy the book. The lady I asked was Sue's friend, but I did not know that. I explained why I wanted the book, and her expression turned sad upon hearing about Sue's death. She hugged me, checked with her boss and they gave me the book at no charge. This book is now in a sealed bag with Sue's other things she had with her the day she went to Heaven.

I have always wondered if the doctor's assistant was with Sue when she had the heart attack. Was she alone? I also believe the two Covid vaccines she had received caused her heart issue. Why? Because she did not have any heart issues prior to the shot and neither did I. After the shot, I have had upper chest pains from time to time, but my examinations could find no cause for these uncomfortable spasms. It may be a coincidence, but neither of us had many health issues prior to the shots. Afterwards, we had many, but only Sue died. I wish I had died, and Sue remained alive.

CHAPTER 27

EXTREME GRIEF AND MORE COMFORTING SIGNS

The week following Susan's death was one of unbearable pain and anguish. Being in our home, surrounded by her decorative magic, reminded me of just how much Susan made this house our home for twenty-three years. I am a strong person, but I drifted into weakness without a loving captain by my side. I thought by getting out of the house for a week or more, I could find some balance. I was also obsessed with choosing the perfect urn for Susan's ashes. I traveled to Tulsa, the week of June 18th, to escape my local torment. I had no intention of going on this trip, even though I had planned it prior to May 26th. Eventually I went anyway, thinking a break was necessary for my sanity. Someone would have to go there to help the Thor Guard team. It may as well be me!

I would divide my time in Tulsa between installing a new system at a stadium, replacing a sensor in another stadium, and providing analytical advisory services to a school. The new team I trained was excellent. Unfortunately, every moment I was not working, I was in constant pain. Every funeral home I drove by or emergency vehicle I encountered brought back pain and tears. My plans for some beneficial escape failed miserably!

The week before Susan died, and before my previous trip to Tulsa, I fell on our lanai, crushing my right foot and toes. This is how I fall when my bad knee gives out without notice. During the fall, I jammed my Seiko watch on a nearby table, breaking the clasp closest to the face of the watch. I was angry but could get it fixed that week. Susan reminded me I was lucky that I broke nothing more than the watch. She was always positive and right!

My first training session in Tulsa schools was for a new installation. The job went well, and the new installer did a great job. Unfortunately, for seemingly no reason, my watch broke again, in the same place, and fell twenty feet onto a stadium seat. That evening, I could again get it repaired. All I could remember was how caring Susan was after I fell on our lanai weeks earlier. Was this just a coincidence? I thought it was. I went back to my hotel to continue my search for the perfect urn.

Susan enjoyed wearing her purple Holy Cross T-shirt, so the urn would be purple. I was looking for an urn with an embracing angel and an orchid. Susan loved orchids and had both white and purple orchids on our lanai. I could not find an urn with an orchid. I purchased a simpler urn with only an angel and had to find someone to add a painted white orchid. This was a sad and difficult process, but nothing was too difficult for my princess.

I took Memorial Road back to the airport from my hotel, rather than my usual route on the interstate.

About halfway to the airport, I noticed a women's clothing store in a strip mall. The store was Sassy's, the same name as Susan's store back in Illinois. Was this another sign from Susan or just a coincidence? I did not know for sure, but suddenly there were so many signs I had to wonder. Were these small encounters messages she was alive in Heaven? I had never been a believer in signs, but my mind was beginning to question my old ways of thinking. I wondered if there would be more signs and how significant they might be.

Upon returning home, I had to arrange for Susan's cremation and begin looking for someone who would paint a flower on the urn. I discussed my options with Susan's daughter Kim, and she told me that a lifelong friend living nearby in Ft. Myers was an accomplished artist. Susan's daughter Kim introduced me to Stacie Krupa, who agreed to do the job for me. Stacie grew up with Kim and knew Susan well. The three of us met at a studio in Naples, so Kim and I could give Stacie the urn and explain what I wanted. Done deal? Not quite.

After a few days, Stacie called me, and we met so I could take possession of Susan's urn. Stacie told me she sat down to paint but stopped because her hands were shaking too hard to continue. She said she was so nervous, not wanting to make a mistake, that she prayed to Jesus for steady hands. Her words were, "like a miracle, my hands stopped shaking, and I completed the orchid". The results of her brilliance and talent were on awesome display, as the orchid painting was perfect. Driving home, I accepted that events occurring around me were far more than coincidences. I did not know at this time how many more of these blessings, as I call them now, would interrupt and bless my daily life.

The last week of June, I had planned to travel to Wisconsin for the US Senior Open at Sentry World in Steven's Point. This was another opportunity to escape Marco Island and the sadness I was living with every day. I stayed for a few days at the event, mostly visiting Thor Guard's resident meteorologist Bryan Conrad and USGA Director John Bodenhamer, before driving to Roselle, Illinois to have breakfast with Anne, Susan's sister. I knew this visit with Anne would be unbearable. I would later fly back home on Saturday afternoon.

I got to my hotel in Janesville, Wisconsin, around 4:30 PM, intending to immediately go to the lobby to print my boarding pass for the next day. For some strange reason, I turned the television on around 4:55 and began channel surfing. I stopped on a channel airing In Fisherman, a program I always watched while I lived in Chicago. There were only five minutes left of the show, but I watched it anyway. To my amazement, the show star, Al Linder, was talking about sitting with his mother as she quietly and peacefully died and moved on. His description of her words of goodbye and love made me wish I had that small piece of time with Susan as she passed. The Linder families' faith was so strong that they knew she was now in Heaven. This provided more reinforcement in my belief that Susan was also in Heaven.

I no longer believed these events and signs were coincidences. They were part of God's plan for me to see and feel. Although I was still grief struck, the faith I had long held close to my heart was being reinforced. I returned home and tried to get my life back together. I realized the task would be impossible in the short term.

I was feeling a bit out of sorts because I had no other signs until July 14th. On that day, I had a service call at Eagle Creek Golf Club, a course Susan and I frequently played. I knew this visit would be very difficult and emotional because I knew every hole on which I drove the cart would fill my mind with good memories. There were no issues with the remote horns on the Thor Guard system, so I drove back to the clubhouse hoping to slip away to my car, seeing none of my friends. As I came to the end of the ninth hole about to turn into the parking lot, there to my right was a beautiful red cardinal just looking at me. I thanked Susan for the sign, and the cardinal flew away. Oddly, I somehow felt Susan was there with me. This was the first sign I had encountered in weeks. I was sad and happy at the same time.

I believed it was time to donate Susan's clothes. It is a tough decision to acknowledge she was not coming home to wear them ever again. I was not emotionally prepared to make that decision, so I delayed it. Instead, I donated my own clothes that were old or too large for me to wear. I started with shirts, some dress pants and jeans. In the following days, I went to my sock drawer to get rid of a bag full of socks, some I had never worn. When I had emptied the drawer, I found a card that simply read "Love" on the cover of the card. I had always saved every card I gave to Susan, and she gave to me, in a box in my office, starting in 1993. I had never seen this card and did not know how it got into this drawer.

Inside the card, a Valentine's Day card, she noted it was our 9th Valentine's Day together, dated 2001. The card's script was "Nobody has ever measured, even poets, how much love a heart can hold", by Zelda Fitzgerald. The card read, "Wishing you a Valentine's Day full of love". Then I read Susan's message to me, "My greatest memory, our first night together, always loving you, Susan". After over thirty years together, I never knew this was something Susan held in her heart. I am still perplexed about why she would bury this card where I was unlikely to ever find it. Why would I find it after she was dead? This will remain a mystery I will never understand.

Samantha, Susan's granddaughter, lives in Burbank, California. Susan would visit Samantha and her daughter Deborah's family every year. There was a bakery called

Porto's, that they would frequent for their delicious bear claws. Everyone loved them, including me. Susan would always bring a few back to me from her trip. During Susan's last visit in 2022, she wore a striped shirt with black pants to Porto's, while getting my goodies before she left for home.

On July 16th, Samantha went to Porto's for a snack and saw Susan's reflection in the glass entry door of the bakery. She was wearing the same striped shirt and dark pants that she wore on the last day of her visit. Samantha said she looked so real that she went to the door to open it for Susan. Susan was not there. This confused Samantha. She does not have a firm belief in Heaven, or maybe even God. We discussed this on the day of Susan's service. To me, it was another sign to her family that Sue was secure in Heaven and watching over all of us. It was also a call for Samantha to believe in God and Heaven. At least, that is how I interpreted the vision.

The weeks following Susan's passing, friends sent me books to read. The first book I had received months prior to Susan's passing was "UFO of God", sent to me by Sue Thomas. She thought I would like it because I watched "Skinwalker Ranch". I read this book after I read "Heaven", by Randy Alcorn, sent to me by my friend Jake Swick (Thor Guard VP). Five hundred pages of positive messaging and an opinion, based on his interpretation of scripture, that Heaven is real and more like a perfect Earth than we could ever imagine.

Richard Varnes, a friend and evangelist, provided the third book. "The Unseen Realm" by Michael Heister was the most confusing book I have ever tried to read. Halfway through, I skipped to the last chapter and understood the book's intention. My neighbor, Sue Thomas, also sent the last book I read. "Signs" by Laura Lynne Jackson, was amazing. Her ability to communicate with those who have died made me think. I was uncertain that Jesus would approve of my interest in the book, but as things would emerge over the next few weeks, I am convinced that this was a book I needed to read.

The next hurdle for me would be on July 20th in Orlando for Susan's memorial mass.

Susan's memorial Mass took place at the Mary Magdalene Catholic church. Kim and Susan's sister Theresa worked with the church to iron out the details. Deborah, Susan's daughter from California, created the video of Susan's life, along with three songs Susan and I loved. The background music included "Somewhere in Time", "Time in a Bottle" and "You Raise Me Up". Watching the history of her life, her life with me and her family, along with that music, made me wonder how I could survive the holy service.

There were about one hundred friends and family in attendance. Many came from out of state, including guests from Illinois, Wisconsin, California and New York. To me, it was like reliving the day Susan died all over again. We lit candles for Susan and honored her in the beautiful urn, embracing her ashes. After the mass, we went to Theresa's (Susan's sister) home for the reception, then back to Kim's. The next day, I returned with Susan to Marco Island.

July 22nd would mark the beginning of an incredible number of signs that changed my perception of Heaven and earth forever.

CHAPTER 28

SIGNS AND MIRACLES FROM JESUS, SUSAN AND MY ANGELS

These last chapters were the only reasons that prompted me to write this book. I never wanted to write about me and my past. My deal with Jesus, on the last Friday in August, was for me to write the book about my past victories and challenges to help guide my readers to more fulfilling lives. Then, write about the signs and miracles I have experienced after Susan died. This is God's portion of my task.

I realize many people will say these events were imagined or are just common coincidences of nature.

For most of my life, I would have taken that position as well. I have now learned in a most painful way, there truly is a living Jesus who loves everyone, even me. For some odd reason, He has chosen me to write about the things I have seen, and things Susan's daughter has seen. The narrative for this chapter is longer than most. That is a requirement to explore each important event and its context.

These last few chapters have been difficult for me to write. The memories of Susan's death and my extended grief are still distressing. I will do the best I can to make this chapter perfect, to return a favor to Jesus, the highest authority who helped me along this long and winding road.

To be clear, every sign and miracle (as I have defined them), is described exactly as observed, experienced and perceived. Neither Susan's daughter Kim nor I have had any dreams that could have been included in this chapter. Every event has a physical, earthly foundation except one. That one is the prompting from Jesus to write this book.

SIGNS AND MIRACLES FROM JESUS, SUSAN AND MY ANGELS

August 9th: I made a trip to Iowa to work with Iowa State University to replace a TG 360 that stopped working. Apparently, the cable that was conduit got damaged from water filling the conduit. The work to replace the cable was successful. I stayed overnight near the college and drove to Des Moines the next day for another night's stay before my trip home the following day.

That evening after dinner, I was in my room, distressed. I was so used to calling Susan while I was away that the absence of a phone call got to me. Around 7:30 PM, I went outside for a cigarette. There were picnic tables in an open area with a few trees surrounding them. I sat beneath a tree and cried. I begged Susan to send me a sign to let me know she was OK. Almost immediately, a yellow butterfly began flying over my head. I watched this one and only butterfly for about fifteen minutes before it flew away. I had read in the book "Signs" that when a cry for help is responded to in some way, you thank that person, so in this case I thanked Susan. The crying did not stop, but I knew that butterfly, in all its beauty, was my sign she was OK.

August 19th: Kim and I went to the 4:30 PM mass at the Divine Mercy Catholic Church in Merritt Island Fl. Kim had not been to church for some time. Susan always wanted Kim to attend mass, but Kim could find a million reasons not to go.

We sat in a pew across from an elderly couple. The woman had Alzheimer's and seemed to be in a comatose state. Her husband was rubbing her back with beautiful love and affection. The mass began and when the Gospel was about to be read, I received a powerful message from Susan to tell Kim she was happy to see her at church and that she loved us both dearly. I began to tell Kim, but Susan told me to wait until after the Gospel was read. I waited as directed and told Kim Susan's message. We both began crying! After a short while, I asked Susan to send me a sign to prove to me I did not make up this thought. Within a minute, the lights in the church flashed for about ten seconds. Those lights have not flashed again in all ten masses I have attended. I was stunned, but more was about to come.

After communion, the server came back to the elderly couple across from us and tried to give the host to the woman. She did not react at all. The server then gave the host to her husband, and he tried for more than a minute with no luck. I looked at the cross and spoke, out loud, "Jesus, if you are really here, please help this woman accept Your body". Almost immediately, she looked at her husband, took the host in her hand and ate it. After eating the host, she looked ahead with no expression on her face. Kim looked at me in amazement and a couple behind us reacted as well. I later told Kim that this was a message for both of us, that Jesus is with us and listens. I refer to this incident as a miracle.

August 22nd: Marriott holds the annual Marriott Golf Con (Convention) for golf management staff worldwide and Marriott Golf and hotel suppliers. Thor Guard has been involved with this event for many years. I initially decided not to attend this year because I did not have the heart to go. Many close friends who work with Marriott Golf knew Susan had died and insisted I reconsider my decision. I attended because I believed that being with other people who knew about Susan might help. I did not want to hide behind my grief any longer. I was supposed to visit my best friend Joe in Scottsdale to get away from Marco, but he came down with Covid, and I delayed my trip until August 21st.

The next day was the golf event. A five-man scramble with many strange games wrapped in the competition. Not having played golf since the week before Susan died, I knew I it would be difficult to participate. It was! I was riding with a golf director from the Grand Cayman Islands, and we began discussing some serious stuff, in between the laughter of our group. I guess a tear fell from one of my eyes and he asked if I was OK. I told him about Susan, and he said he was sorry. I said it was OK because of the signs I had already experienced. He asked about them. I then asked if he was a Christian and he responded 'yes'. I then asked if he was Catholic, and he replied, 'sort of'. I understood and related some signs I had experienced. He told me about a childhood friend who had cancer. The patient had moved to a distant, new hospital, so frequent visits were difficult. On his last visit in October, his friend told him not to cry because on December 22nd, he would come home. My friend was relieved and returned home expecting to see his friend soon. On December 22nd, his friend died, confirming his vision. At that point, my new friend understood his dying friend meant he was going to Heaven. We were both speechless, but grateful we had that conversation, playing golf, of all things!

August 23rd: I left for my hotel at the airport for the night. I had a 5:55 AM flight back to Orlando, where Kim would pick me up and go back to her home. With such an early flight, I went to dinner early and tried to go to sleep around 8 PM. I could not sleep. Around 9 PM, I had a strange yearning for orange juice. I never drink juice after breakfast! I initially decided not to go to the lobby for juice, something told me to go. I got dressed, grabbed my cigarettes, and went to the lobby to find the last orange juice in the cooler. I grabbed it and went to the front desk to pay. The receptionist said, "Hi, my name is Susan. Should I charge this to your room?" I was shocked and thought her being another Susan was the reason for the juice craving. I was very wrong!

I went outside to have my juice and one cigarette or more. In the smoking area was a man in his fifties smoking some strange cigarette. I asked what it was, and he said it was a Peruvian smoke. He asked if I wanted one. I said no thank you, I will stick with my plain ones from America. We began talking at 9:10 PM and learned he grew up near Worcester, Massachusetts, where I attended college. We spoke of restaurants, fishing and the area. I then asked why he was in Phoenix. He said he changed jobs to be with his dying father. I asked where he was working, and he said NOAA. I asked what division, and he said storm and atmospheric prediction analysis. An amazing alignment of our fields. I informed him that his division does forecasting, not prediction. I told him about Thor Guard. He was very interested and excited to learn about our technology, technology which he referred to as 'AI'. Towards the end of my impromptu class on lightning and storm prediction, I began to tear up again. He saw this and asked me if I was OK. I told him about Susan, and he said, "I am sorry for your loss".

I asked the same two questions as I asked the golf pro the day before and got the same answers!

Amazing! I told him of some signs I had encountered. After I was done, he told me that two of his best friends in North Carolina, both professors, were interested in the hereafter. One had died and come back and the other studied clairvoyants. Now this was becoming too weird. He thanked me for the conversation and at 11 PM I told him I had an early flight and needed to go to sleep. He asked if I had a business card, but I didn't. Steve and I shook hands and said goodnight. I was walking away, and he asked me to come back. I returned, and he told me he had no intention of going out for a cigarette that evening, but something told him he would meet someone very important in his life. We believe it was God's intention that I was that person. We parted ways, and I went back to my room. After this encounter, there was no sleep in my immediate future. My mind was spinning!

CHAPTER 29

A NOT-SO-SUBTLE ORDER FROM JESUS

S usan died a little over three months ago. Each Friday brings pure sadness to my life. I find no escape from the anguish I experience, no matter what actions I take to ease this pain. I take sleeping aids to fall asleep every night. Sometimes they work and other times they fail. The evening of August 24th would be one of those nights. Nothing worked. Instead, I completely broke down in tears. I pleaded with God and Jesus to tell me why I was left to live without my princess. Through heavy tears, I explained my determination to keep Thor Guard operational, with the goal of saving more lives. But there had to be something more that He wanted from me. I eventually fell asleep around 11 PM. I have had no dreams since Susan died, and this night would be no different. That all changed at 1:30 AM the next morning.

I abruptly woke up to what I recall as a loud gunshot sound. I sat up and received the answer to my prayerful plea hours earlier. Jesus told me I would write the book I never wanted to write. However, he told me the book would not be the one I had dismissed but would be quite different. He said the first part of the book would be the same as I may have written, but the second part will be unlike anything I could have imagined. He wanted me to provide an accurate account of all the signs and miracles I experienced since May 26th. I foolishly advised Him I had never written a book, and that if I accepted this challenge, He would have to help me every step of the way. I had authored articles on lightning and weather safety measures, but nothing of the scope of a project like this. Especially with the pressure I would undoubtedly experience because these marching orders came directly from Jesus, my Savior. He agreed to help me, and as a result, I experienced His help every step along this journey. Before every chapter, I reminded Him He promised to help, and He responded every time. One time I was beginning Chapter Three, I intentionally did not pray, as a test. I sat there for half an hour with no idea what to write. I eventually prayed, and the memories and words appeared like magic in my head. That was the last time I ever sat down to write where I did not pray.

That early morning revelation has changed my perspective on life and the beliefs I have taken for granted since I was born. I pray He will be happy with the results of our collaborative writing.

MORE SIGNS AND MIRACLES

August 28th: Around 7:58 PM, Kim was sad after talking to Susan next to a porcelain angel statue on the pool deck. She spoke into her phone (Siri) saying, "Hi, I love and miss you mom". Immediately, a text came back with a background picture of Kim and her mom. Beneath the picture were the words "You are the wind beneath my wings". That song was played at Susan's memorial mass. How would Siri know this?

Kim and I believed the message came directly from Susan. It was a challenge to provide any other logical explanation.

September 3rd: This was just another sad Sunday without my best friend. I sat on the lanai and spoke to Susan as if she was sitting next to me. I told her I needed another sign that she was hearing me and somehow alive in a place that permitted her to communicate with those she left behind. Once again, a beautiful butterfly landed on the screen for about ten minutes. Susan loved butterflies, so I am not surprised she uses these lovely, delicate, and beautiful creatures to respond to my pleas. I thanked her again for providing me with another sign, at which time the butterfly flew away, never to be seen again. As you will see as I recount more of these special signs, and my constant need for more, I am a very needy person. I never knew how needy until now!

September 16th: I was back at Kim's house this weekend and again, we attended the 4:30 PM mass at Divine Mercy church. We sat in the same pew we did at the previous mass, directly across from the elderly couple. As usual, he was lovingly rubbing his wife's back as she sat there in a comatose state. After communion, the server brought him the host for his wife's consumption, and as previously observed, she did not react. This time, I waited several minutes, hoping she would turn to her husband and take the holy communion. She did not. Once again, I asked Jesus just one more time to help this lady accept His body and on cue; she turned to her husband, took the host in her hand, ate it, then returned to her catatonic state. I thanked God, amazed at His willingness to help, again!

November 2nd: There was a remembrance mass for all the people from Mary Magdalene church who had either died in 2023 or had a service for a past loved one held at the church. Kim and I attended the service to honor Susan. We both knew that attending would be difficult, and it was as difficult as we had feared.

We both received communion and were returning to our pews when Kim looked at me in amazement and had me stop and listen to the music being played. This mass was in both English and Spanish. The guitarist was singing, and the words were as clear as day, sung multiple times, "Susan Diane". Susan's full name is Susan Diane Dugan. We were both in shock! I later asked the woman who managed this mass if these were Spanish words we could not understand. She was aghast and uncertain. We were also emotionally moved as well!

November 12th: I was having another terribly sad day on an otherwise beautiful Sunday morning. I asked Susan why she had not sent me any signs since August. I was not thinking about the book, only wishing for a new, fresh sign. Suddenly, the name of my book just popped into my head. Prior to that, I did not know what to call my book. I went inside and wrote down the book's new title, then returned to the lanai and thanked Susan for the title and the sign. Immediately, a beautiful butterfly appeared on the screen. The colors were unique, with red wings and black dots. I can honestly tell you I never see butterflies around our home on Marco. Never!

November 13th: I called Kim in the evening to say that I received another message from Susan. Susan wanted me to tell Kim that she loved us both and that she was with us. The message perplexed Kim. Then we both cried. While these messages are uplifting, they are sad because each one reminds us that Susan is no longer with us in person.

November 14th: There is a recliner in Kim's living room, along with a sofa with a recliner at one end. Susan would always sit on this sofa / recliner to read or watch TV with the foot section raised. This was her spot! The morning after my last call, Kim went into the living room to turn the television on for the dog and noticed the recliner footrest was raised. Kim thought this was strange because no one sat on this sofa. She lowered it and left the house to go shopping. When she returned, the footrest was again in the raised position. She called me a little scared and returned it to the lower position. Before bed, she went into the room to turn the television off and, once again, the footrest was raised. She lowered it again and called me to tell me it happened again. I told her to accept the fact this was a message from her mom. Be grateful and tell your mom you love her. That evening was the last time the footrest was raised!

November 21st: I drove from my office to spend Thanksgiving with Kim and Hailey, her daughter. I cooked prime ribs for dinner. Kim and I baked a rhubarb pie, messing it up the first time around, but got it right the second time. The dinner was superb and just sharing this time together on our first Thanksgiving without Susan, made the holiday bearable. The rest of the week was one of love and great sadness, but we survived.

I got up early on November 27th to drive to the office at 7 AM, a three-hour drive. As I opened the front door to go to my car, there was a beautiful butterfly with, as you may have guessed, beautiful red wings with black dots. Seeing the same-colored butterfly three hundred miles from Marco Island made me realize Susan was with us and wanted Kim and me to know it. I finally knew, even with the numerous signs and other events I had experienced, that Susan was indeed with us all the time.

November 29th: With so many mysterious things happening, Kim asked Susan for another sign, just for her. She left the house for the grocery store and took a right turn on Courtney Road, the major north-south street through Merritt Island. As she approached the first stoplight, in front of her was a black SUV from Georgia. The car's license tag was "Heaven". For those of you non-believers, what are the odds of both Kim and I seeing that license tag from different states exactly when a sign was needed?

I know some math and I can say the odds are astronomical, especially when they come at the very moment a sign is needed most!

December 10th: Kim was depressed and not eating well. Whenever I visited, we would eat together because I love eating, even though I had lost ten pounds since Susan left me. After I leave, Kim returns to poor eating habits. I told her she needed to eat better and have a healthy dinner every night.

This evening, she placed some leftover spaghetti in the microwave and went to the lanai to call her daughter in California. They spoke for some time, then Kim realized the food was still in the microwave. She hung up with Samantha and went to the kitchen. Kim was alone because Hailey was working. She was surprised to find the food on the counter and not in the microwave. Kim assumed she had forgotten to put the spaghetti in the microwave and thought she was losing her mind! She went to pick up the food to place it in the microwave for cooking, but to her bewilderment; it was fully cooked. Another mystery? Perhaps. Susan is acting as the watchful mom she has always been.

CHAPTER 30

CHRISTMAS DAY -
MESSAGES FROM
HEAVEN

December 25th: This would be the first Christmas Day,
Susan's favorite holiday, without her.

Kim and I agreed to help one another through our first
Christmas without Susan. We both knew this would be a
very sad and challenging time.

We would divide our day between visiting Kim's
daughter, Kaytlin, and Susan's family in Orlando.

These visits would be a blessing, as they kept our minds
occupied and took some of the loneliness from the day. Early
that morning, as the sun rose, I was having a cigarette on the
lanai with my early morning coffee. I wished Susan a Merry
Christmas, trying to imagine how wonderful this day was
in Heaven. For the first time since I had seen a cardinal at
Eagle Creek, a very red cardinal landed on the fence and sat
there for a minute. Once again, Susan came to the rescue,
letting me know she was with us in spirit. This would be the
beginning of a truly remarkable day!

We returned home about 6:30 PM; I was exhausted after the long drive and visits. Kim went to her bedroom to watch TV, and I stayed in the living room, deciding to watch The Chosen (Season 3, Episode 8). I watched every episode from home on my DVR. I hate commercials, so recording the episodes allowed me to fast forward to the good stuff. This was the episode where Jesus broke the bread and fish to feed the thousands there to listen to his sermons. Afterwards, He ordered Simon to take the apostles across the Sea of Galilee to beat the incoming storm. Of course, they parted company and later, the boat was in the middle of the storm and sinking. Jesus appeared from nowhere and walked to them on the water. That is when Jesus ordered Simon to come to him and walk on the water. Simon was scared but did what Jesus asked of him. He got close to Jesus and was told to forget the waves and wind and watch Jesus's eyes. Simon did not listen and sank below the surface of the water. Jesus reached down, grabbed his hand, and saved Simon. The two went back to the boat, a boat that was sinking because of the storm, and Jesus told the storm to stop. His orders were followed.

After watching the show, I went to the lanai to have a cigarette and talk some more to Susan. In my overly emotional state-of-mind, I began talking to Jesus. I was crying hard! I had read so often that Jesus is sad when we are. I asked Him if he cries when we cry. It began to rain. It had not rained all day at the house. I then asked Him if he cried as hard as I was crying, then it began to pour. At this point, I felt like I was with Jesus and had Him all to myself. I literally told Him I did not want Him crying for me and that I promised I would do my best to stop. To my unexpected amazement, the rain stopped immediately. It never rained again that evening. He was with me. I still cry more than I want, but less than before.

The pain I experienced, missing my princess on Christmas Day, was excruciating. That evening, while sitting in Kim's living room, before I watched The Chosen, I texted Susan a message. I knew her phone had not been on since the day she died, but I continued to pay for her service because I wanted to occasionally call to hear her recorded voice on the phone. At 7:42 Pm, I texted: "Merry Christmas my love. I miss you so much. I love you forever". At 7:42 PM, I received a return text that read: "I love you more". From her cell phone! I still have that call sequence on my cell phone,

Insert Screen shot of text from Susan.

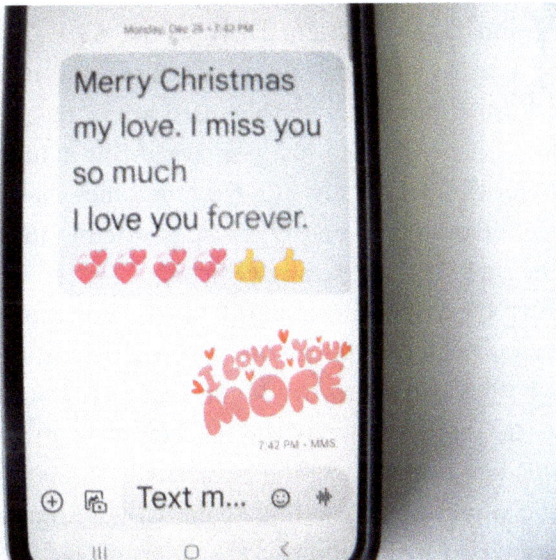

Text from Susan

CHAPTER 31

2024-A NEW YEAR AND NEW MESSAGES

January 19th, 2024: Early in the week, I was watching a replay of a "48 Hours" TV show about the murder of a husband by his wife. She used a 357 magnum to do the job. I have watched many shows of this nature, but the 357 number stuck in my mind. Three times that week I would see the time 3:57 on my car clock when I randomly checked the time, and on passing vehicles.

On Friday afternoon, January 19th, Kim had a second deposition being forced on her when the insurance company, who has refused to pay for serious neck injuries suffered in a rear-ender five years ago, selected new attorneys after her doctor's deposition. She was very nervous and concerned she would not do well. I couldn't figure out what could be associated with number 357, and it was really bothering me. I wondered if this related to some Bible verse and if so, how might it apply to me? Son of a gun, there it was. I believe it was a message for Kim that I had to share with her. On that Friday morning, as she was driving to her lawyer's office to prepare for the deposition, I read it to her and specifically told her this message was just for her. 'Lamentations, 3:57, 58 and 59: "You came near when I called and You said, do not fear". 58: "You, Lord, took up my cause. You redeemed my life". 59: "Lord, You have seen the wrong done to me. Uphold my cause". Kim did a great job in the deposition. I felt lucky that I had my eyes and mind open to more signs from above. However, at least for that moment in time, Kim was the intended recipient of this one.

January 21st, 2024: The PGA show was the following week. For the first time without Susan on our annual trip to the show, I would instead drive to my Sunrise, Florida, office to pick up some show supplies, then to my hotel room by Bass Pro Shops in Dania Beach. I would later meet my friend and corporate lawyer, Andrew Gordon, for dinner. Halfway across Alligator Alley, US Route 75, I stopped for a cigarette break. The many memories of my past trips to Orlando with Susan finally got to me. I tried to keep my promise to Jesus to cut the crying out, but to no avail. Instead, I expressed my appreciation for helping me write the book and the many signs I have been blessed with for the first few months. I finished a cigarette and looked up at the sky. I should not have been surprised, but I saw two very large angel wings perfectly formed by the clouds. Again, I thanked Jesus and Susan for the uplifting reminder I was not alone.

January 27th: The week of the PGA show, I brought a framed picture of Susan and me on our wedding day. I needed to bring her along, as I had done for many years. After returning to Kim's for the weekend, I placed all my clothes and the picture in the guest bedroom where I always stayed. It is a totally dark room at night. As I was getting into bed, I glanced at the picture and there was, for a moment, a bright light on Susan's face. The reflection of my face wasn't visible on the picture's glass, even though I was right next to it. I knew she was with me that evening!

Today is February 11th, the day before the thirty-first anniversary of our meeting at Studebaker's. We always had a special dinner somewhere to celebrate. I bought flowers for our February 12th anniversary, planning to spend the evening with my princess, well sort of. She cannot attend because she is in Heaven. As of today, there have been no additional signs Kim and I have experienced. However, I know there will be many more to come, especially when we really need one!

.

CHAPTER 32

ALL I AM

WHAT I HAVE LEARNED

I consider the first forty years of my life to be comparable to what some refer zto as "Helter Skelter". Personally, and professionally, I was nowhere and everywhere. I was most likely on some mis-guided path of destruction. Clearly, God had a unique plan for me and guided me through the wild distractions of my mind and my actions.

I spent a great deal of time thinking about and writing these last few chapters. I am grateful God had a plan and made certain I would follow His wishes and quiet suggestions. These chapters, as difficult as they were to write and read many times over, serve as a constant reminder that His plan for me did not include failure. I guess in a convoluted way; I learned so many of life's lessons in ways few will experience. I will do my best to share these lessons so you can be guided to complete fulfillment in your life, if that is possible. I share these thoughts and experiences with you as a friend, perhaps a new friend. Hopefully, your understanding of my past will help you in your life's journey.

I am certain you have as many, if not more, experiences in your life that seem as crazy or insignificant as my own. Learning is never easy and the more thought you put into your efforts, the more you will learn and discover. As you read this last chapter, try to relate my growth and beliefs to my experiences. Think about which of those experiences formed who I am, then look at your own past and do the same. It is never too late to change for the better, if you are willing. We all know that there is no guarantee for tomorrow, so take today and discover the best you can be now. Once you embrace life's journey and consider all you have experienced, you may find a better and more loving person inside. Perhaps a great person who has been inside for a long time. If so, let them out!

When I think about some of my favorite shows from the past, each one involves time travel. Time travel or getting beamed-up involves going from one place to another faster than light will travel through space. One might call this perfectly efficient transportation! As I have taken this nostalgic trip remembering every detail of my life, one theme continues to recur. From the day I was born to this very moment in 2024, my time on earth seems to have passed more quickly than any Star Trek form of intergalactic travel. The nine months since Susan's death have thankfully passed as quickly.

The extent to which your life is filled with both good and bad experiences does not matter. Never waste your time doing something you don't enjoy, especially a career, because the time you spend being miserable will never be recovered. Don't allow failure or grief to overwhelm your life with negativity. Never put off sharing a hug, kiss or kind word with someone because that opportunity may never present itself again. Remember, time is your enemy!

The only control you have in your life is to embrace the choices that determine what your future should look like, using experiences and possibly those small subliminal suggestions as a guide to future decisions. Always try to remember that some event or injury that you perceive as bad or tragic in your life may be a blessing in disguise. The damage caused by holding onto negativity in your life is enormously destructive. I am an expert on this subject!

I always believed that my life was difficult compared to some other people. Now that I have truly examined my past, I realize I exacerbated some difficulties I experienced by cursing at God for causing each one. I now realize that these difficulties were carefully disguised blessings.

For instance, the first tragedy in my life was contracting juvenile polio. Had I not had polio, I would most likely have been a professional athlete in a sport of my choosing. My arrogance and narcissism would have helped me excel in athletics but would have encouraged the deep seated demon that had made me a terrible person. Polio eliminated any chance of a successful career in professional sports. With polio and a life away from professional athletics, my life's mission as directed by God became reality. I believe that having polio made me work harder than anyone else just to prove my bad leg would not be the reason for failure.

I think of all the wonderful people I have met in my life, the fantastic golf and skiing trips, my incredible life with Thor Guard and a once-in-a-lifetime soulmate with whom I shared thirty-one years of perfect love and friendship. Saying that I was blessed would be an understatement. In retrospect, there are many others whose lives are and were far more difficult than my own. For me, the most challenging emotion to overcome and defeat is that automatic response to any unfair event that made me feel sorry for myself. Eliminating these negative emotions, far harder said than done, has improved my life and brought me peace.

Remember that terrible temper I always carried around as a first response to anything that went bad? Those outbursts were a complete waste of time and effort. They never contributed to anything positive in my life. Now that this demon is no longer a part of my existence, I am a much happier person.

The day Susan died and the way she died with no advance notice was devastating. If I carried that old, uncontrolled temper around with me today, I would have completely lost it and blamed Jesus for cruelly taking her away from me. After all, I know He put us together but taking her away before I was ready felt wrong.

In my new sense of understanding, I did not curse God or Jesus. I simply cried and asked that He take good care of my princess and help me get through what I knew was going to be the most difficult time of my life.

Even though my lifelong relationship with God was, at times, contentious, the help and sometimes miraculous intervention from Jesus clearly reveals that He never left me! His love for every one of us is more encompassing than we can imagine. This is an undeniable fact. I wish I had embraced this understanding sixty years ago. I also understand that if I had, perhaps I would not be where I am today. This further reinforces my belief that the offensive actions, poor decisions and negative thoughts in my life were a necessary part of my life's path forward.

The moment one stops learning and listening to these quiet suggestions, he or she stops improving and from that point in life on, achieving complete success and true happiness is unlikely! I find it strange how things perceived as bad at different times in my life were potentially good, but only to the degree that I moved forward and placed that experience into the "life's lesson bucket". Use them all for yourself and others. Don't let them use you!

I believe that before a new soul is sent to earth, God has a complete life plan for it. Some may call it fate! God's objective is that the soul becomes a happy and successful part of a great society and eventually achieves whatever God desires. I also believe, because it is exactly how I arrived at this point in my life, that God and His angels are always providing spiritual suggestions, perhaps not obvious, but sometimes blatantly physical, to guide us along the most desired path. Because we are humans with free will, we will drift off course into potentially disastrous waters.

These brief messages, like the one that insisted I go to Costa Rica for that fishing trip, are intended to correct a potentially bad course of action a person may pursue or help discover a better one. Or the time I had given up finding a woman to be my life partner, then gave a cookie to that pretty girl who would become the most important person in my life. I am now certain that there were hundreds or thousands of other suggestions that guided me along the way, permitting me to land where I am today.

People will undoubtedly dismiss this notion of a plan set in motion by God at birth, but contrary to these naysayers' beliefs, I believe that the only way to live a truly happy and fulfilling life is to listen to these Heavenly messages and follow the leads, wherever they go. The only entity that wants a human to be directed away from God's personal plan for a happy existence on earth is, are you ready? The devil. He exists. How do I know? He tried to force me to lose my love for Jesus by enticing me to blame Him for Susan's death. There was a day in my past that blaming anyone would be the easy way to deal with this tragedy. For more than a month, the Lord's Prayer became the battleground as the devil tried to interrupt my prayer with terrible, ugly, and hateful thoughts towards God. It became so contentious that I finally shouted out loud for the devil to go screw himself! That worked for a short while, but he came back many times.

When I felt him interfering, I would repeatedly tell him where to go. He has not been around for months, but I know he will return to try again. He will fail again!

My friend and Evangelist Richard Varnes did not like my reference to self-hypnosis, inferring some may perceive it as voodoo or evil magic. I was a psychology major in college and later took self-hypnosis courses to overcome my temper. These actions were instrumental in controlling my destructive outbursts! I believe this practice is simply a method of using frequently practiced breathing exercises, feeling a deep meditative experience, perhaps with God, and tying those calming feelings back to the deep breathing exercises when you most need them.

Taking a series of deep breaths helped me manage my temper. I find some personal space, close my eyes and take a deep breath, hold it briefly, then exhale slowly and completely. I will do this same sequence again. The third time is the same, except I exhale as hard as I can. After doing these breathing exercises wherever I was, the calm feelings I had experienced in my meditative, prayerful state comes back.

Today, I embrace achieving this relaxed state to pray. Quieting your mind and focusing your thoughts can truly amaze you at how close you can get to God and Heaven's residents. Whether you use this form of relaxation or some other method of prayer, praying is the most important thing you can do in your life. It provides a greater awareness of these messages intended to help you through life. Prayers also provide calmness and a feeling of wellness crucial to every life experience and may ultimately help you manage the destructive explosions of rage we all encounter from time to time.

I have always prayed, reciting prayers I learned in my younger days. Many people pray with a rosary, some with the Bible and many never pray at all! I would never tell people, even friends, how to pray or for how long. When I stopped reciting prayers and began talking to Jesus in everyday language, this new way to connect brought me closer to understanding who Jesus and God are. I still say some prayers, but my personal time praying is now just having a long chat with my friend. I believe any prayer method is important, particularly if it brings you closer to God. For me and my simpler self, I enjoy just sharing ideas with the Heavenly force in my life that made me into someone I can like. It took me a long time to figure this out. That is, having a relationship with Jesus on a level I can comprehend. One nice part of having a friend who loves me all the time is that I can always reach Him without the internet or a cell phone. Convenient? Absolutely!

Today, I am a far different person than I was thirty-two years ago. I believed I always had a good heart, but my relationships with women were horrible. My attitude towards life was dark. Every effort I put forth was for me. I believed the world revolved around me and my desires; I believed this world owed me, and I lived with a contentious relationship with the only power who could change my life's trajectory. The facts are now clear; I did not have such a good heart after all!

We hear so many times that there is always an exceptional woman behind every great and successful man. I will expand on that to include the fact that there is a great man behind every successful woman. In my case, Susan totally changed every aspect of my life. Sue always loved and supported me. She wanted to be with me. She wanted our time together to be selfishly ours. I felt the same way and grew with her graciousness. Our many close friendships developed along the way, the success I now experience, professionally and personally, resulted from allowing these people into our lives. As valuable to me as each friend was and is, it was Susan who radically altered the trajectory and purpose of my life. She did this with love, care, and affection. Susan always welcomed my friends into our home with open arms. Then they became "our" friends. She never aggressively pushed any position or opinion on me. Every Saturday or Sunday, there was mass and prayers to God keeping us in line the following week. To each of us, receiving communion was the most important act we embraced every week. I have not missed a mass since May 26th, and each time I receive communion, I am filled with new hope for a better week ahead.

As I have now experienced many times, I am still sad and have difficulty seeing a way out of this deep, dark hole. There are, however, many bright memories that overshadow the tragic loss of Susan. From the day we met, we never left for work or play without sharing a hug and a kiss. We never missed a hug and a kiss when I returned home from work or some trip. Everywhere we went, we always held hands. When we were away from each other on some trip, we would routinely speak with one another three to five times a day. I am so happy that there was never a time our words of love and commitment went unsaid. If we did not live like we really loved and respected each other, and shared those thoughts every day, my life today without Susan would be irretrievably dead. I can't even imagine what that would feel like today.

For those of you with a special love in your life, never let a day pass, even if you have a fight or serious disagreement, that you don't fully and honestly express your love and devotion with your closest friend. You may never get a do over! You never know when your time clock runs out!

ALL I AM

I am not the person I was ten, twenty, thirty, or even seventy years ago. I am grateful for that power that changed the trajectory of my life. Seventy-years of life is a long time. A long span of years that passed in the blink of an eye. Of all the amazing and sometimes imperceptible influences that altered my life that I have relayed to you in this book, no one can hold a candle to the events described in chapters twenty-six through thirty-one. I will never know why He selected me and Kim to experience so many spiritual manifestations, but I am grateful He did.

Both Kim and I have come to a better understanding of the depth of the Lord's love and caring, often in ways we still have a difficult time comprehending. I attended church my entire life. I prayed so many times that I could never innumerate those efforts. It was my belief I was basically a good person with a healthy but contentious relationship with my Creator. A far cry from perfection.

As I sit here today working on closing the last chapter of this book, I can easily see that Jesus planned for me to write this book since the day I was conceived. Remember, I never wanted to write any book about my life and had no intense reason for doing one. He promised me He would be with me and help me with every chapter, and He kept His word. You may not like what I have written or how I interpreted the events of the last eight months. However, my job was to relay these messages and signs to help promote some thoughts and questions on your part, perhaps to rethink the beliefs you have held for years. It will hopefully encourage those who already believe to experience some strengthening in their own life and beliefs, and give those who are undecided some serious food for thought. At least that is what I pray for.

We all have an expiration date. We will never know when or where we will be called back to meet our Creator. For those of us who are older, we know how quickly time flies and that it is impossible to turn back the clock...

I do not know what Jesus has in store for me, if anything. I love my work. I love fishing. I sort of like golf, and I enjoy being with my friends. I know I will miss Susan deeply for the rest of my life and see no room for a replacement in my heart. I look forward to speaking with and counseling more students, now that I have a broader and better understanding of challenging career paths and the Heaven few of us embrace. Some may say my life's journey was destructive, disorganized, yet somehow blessed. Perhaps it was. I am revisiting the early enjoyments I embraced. My love of teaching has become a more important part of my life. I hope I continue to grow. I hope to continue to strive to learn new things and in doing so; I hope I will never fall short of God's aspirations for me.

With the final chapter of my life yet unwritten, who I am today is ALL I AM!

ACKNOWLEDGEMENTS

There are so many individuals I need to thank for their continued support and patience during this trying time in my life. There are not enough words that can adequately express the depth of my appreciation, but in mentioning these friends, I hope that I have expressed my most sincere gratitude. I guess I still do some things my way. I will probably never change every aspect of my life!

Two of my best friends for over forty years, Joe Bush and Jim Rourke, were there from the start, never judging or diverting me from what I knew I needed to do. They listened patiently and carefully to me and said they would support anything I might do in the future. Joe wants me to come to Scottsdale for a week of golf and escape. I look forward to that week. Two other long time friends from Park Ridge, Illinois days, Steve and Jan Meyer, were also there for me. Steve was so overcome by grief that he had a difficult time talking to me. Steve and Jan really loved Susan.

Special thanks to my former lawyer and close friend Cheryl Wilke for editing my manuscript. I know she thought she knew me well, but my guess is that after reading this manuscript, she learned things about me she never knew. Cheryl was also very kind to offer me a weekend escape from Marco at her Boca Raton condominium. Kim and her sister Deborah visited their mom's house to take some of Susan's personal items they wanted for keepsakes. I knew I could not be in the house for that visit. Cheryl's condo escape was perfect!

Jake Swick and Sue Thomas were there for me, as stated in Chapter 29, and provided some excellent books for me to read. I wholeheartedly recommend "Heaven" and "Signs," as they were extraordinarily helpful. Susan's lifelong friends, Myra Gresko and Garrie Senior, were there for me as well. They were thoughtfully supportive and full of marvelous stories of their experiences with Susan. They all continue to check on me from time to time.

Chris Crossan has been visiting me two to three times a week, nearly every week since Susan died. His cheerful face and positive attitude are always uplifting, even on those days I don't want any company. It helps that his faith is strong and has a good family life. Eventually, we will fish and play golf again.

My business partner Peter Townsend and his wife Penny have also been there from day one.

They understood the pain I was living with because they knew how much Susan meant to me. My visit last year to their home in Lake George, New York, was special and a welcome break from Marco Island, a getaway I needed. Business partners being good friends are a difficult pairing to find, especially when I was a handful as a partner. After thirty-three years, I am fortunate to have found them both. Penny also helped with my editing. Thank you, Peter. Thank you, Penny.

Susan's daughter Kim Dilday lived through the same horrible pain as I did, and do, because Kim and Susan were not only mother and daughter, but best friends. We will continue to share the pain of Susan's loss and help one another work through the days, weeks, months and years of sadness that exist in our hearts and souls. For me, Kim was instrumental in helping me cope with my depression and hopelessness. As I explained earlier in the book, I see so much of my Susan in Kim, but with an entirely unique personality. With Kim, I am calm and less sad.

I meet every morning at 6:30 with my morning coffee guys at the Marco Island Dunkin' Donuts. They help me start every day with a smile.

I needed some feedback from friends as I wrote my manuscript. Chapter by chapter, each of these individuals provided me with a useful commentary on everything I was writing. Their comments helped me organize my strategy to bring many themes to a conclusion. My sincerest thanks to Sue Thomas, Jason Wolk, David Redanz, Jake Swick, Kim Dilday, Peter Townsend, Richard Varnes, Joe Raczkowski, Frank McCathran, Chris Crossan, Steve Meyer, Andrew Gordon and Debbie Walsh. God bless you!

Throughout the many hours of writing, the thousands of words written and thousands more words trashed because they weren't perfect, one force remained by my side and would not let me quit. This force has been with me my entire life and until recently, I did not realize how close He really was. Jesus, thank You for believing in me and for not giving up on my wandering soul. Thank You for every word and idea I wrote. I will always look ahead with great anticipation for the day I meet You in person. I hope my efforts have made You happy with me!

EPILOGUE

I have mostly completed everything in "All I Am" for over one month, except for this epilogue. It is now early May 2024, close to one year since Susan left me for Heaven. There are a few final thoughts I need to relate to you, my most valuable reader.

People who have read the book in its pre-publication form have asked me why I received so many signs? Eventually, I realized that without those frequent signs and miracles, I would have had nothing of value to write. Remember, I never wanted to write a book about my life. But during this challenging time, Susan and Jesus kept me in constant amazement, sometimes bewilderment, and overwhelmed my stubborn head with constant reminders that the entire book and its contents were special.

Two days after Easter, 2024, Sue Thomas asked me to come to her house for dinner. She told me that Graciela, her mom and dad, were visiting and wanted me to join them.

Dinner was superb! I love barbeque ribs, coleslaw, potato salad and real baked beans. After dinner, Graciela's dad asked me if I had questions for her. I said no, although I had many. I didn't really want to hear the answers. Graciela began using her tablet to give her mom a message for me, anyway. She informed me that if I could clear my head of earthly distractions, I could talk to my friends and family who have passed. Graciela noticed I was very sad, but that Susan's spirit was there with me. She ended by telling me that Jesus would have me write another book. I was not expecting that!

On April 24th, the day before Susan's birthday, I finally had a dream with Susan in it. This was the first time since she died. In my dream, I had finished speaking to a class of junior and senior high school students at LaSalle. In the top row of the bleachers, where parents and teachers were seated, I noticed a small blonde woman. I was drawn to her. When I was standing below her on the gymnasium floor, I saw this beautiful young girl, some freckles and a sweet smile. She said nothing, but I realized it was Susan in her Heavenly form. No words were spoken, but the communication of love between us was quite clear. This is one dream I will never forget.

Kim and I have, from time to time, smelled Susan briefly in our presence. Never when we are together, but when we are apart in our respective homes. On two occasions at my house, I observed wrinkles on the covering of the sofa where Sue always sat watching TV or reading, as if someone had sat there. I always keep it smooth, and no one visits me and sits there. I guess she is letting me know that her spirit is still around me!

I wish I could say that I was healing nicely, but that would be a lie. I deeply miss my princess every day and wish to have her back or to join her. There are still things that make me happy and laugh, but there is no true joy in my life right now except for the possibility that my story will help others through the grieving process. Friends who have lost their spouses have told me it will be years before any normalcy in my life returns. I guess that is the ultimate cost of losing your life's soulmate. One blessing is that time has passed so quickly that May 26, 2023, seems like yesterday. That must be Jesus' way of helping me cope without Susan.

I am certain you noticed I frequently smoke. Susan would go out on our lanai, before or after dinner, and have a smoke. I wanted to be with her all the time, so I resumed smoking after many years away from that terrible habit. Unfortunately, when I now smoke, it is like I am still doing something special with Susan. In time, that crutch will no longer be necessary. Until that day arrives, I will continue to smoke.

I believe this position needs to be repeated. This life's journey has revealed many things about my life's choices. So many times, I was pointed in a different direction than I was inclined to go. I am where I am today because of these choices. I believe God has a lifelong plan for every soul. His goal is for that soul to live a happy, caring, loving, and successful life. Missteps along the way are forgiven if one returns to the plan from God and keeps Him in one's heart. As it is, I am a perfect example of this. I am so grateful He forgave my indiscretions and loved me as I was and am.

From my perspective, Jesus chose an imperfect author (me), to write an imperfect book for imperfect people. What could possibly go wrong? Absolutely nothing!

Jesus, thank You for believing in me.

Thank you for reading our book. God bless you!